GROUNDED

"Anchor" Management for Strategic Leadership
and Effective Decision-Making

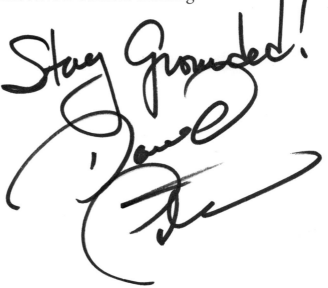

What people are saying

"Fascinating expose on the role of leadership in the wreckage of three sailing ships synthesized to life experience on the high seas of 21st century business. A fast read for those who might not typically pick up a business book!"

— **David Johnson**
Cedar Point Capital

"We cannot let ourselves be grounded by the shipwrecks in our lives. Instead, we must be grounded in traits that allow us to forge onward with courage and wisdom. My own journey from accident victim to Paralympic medalist, entrepreneur, proud husband and father, is no exception, and in the pages of 'Grounded', I found words of encouragement and wisdom suitable for anyone's journey."

— **Bert Burns**
Paralympics Medalist, Founder of LASCI
(Life After Spinal Cord Injury)

"A wise and important book! As a seasoned explorer and professional executive leadership coach, I appreciate the unique value of the management and strategy insights of 'Grounded', wrapped in an exciting adventure story!"

— **Dr. Jeff Salz**
Author of *The Way of Adventure*

"What do shipwrecks have to do with business? Much more than you might think. In 'Grounded', by David Peterson, we discover lessons about the 'anchors' that can help us successfully navigate the crisis situations that we all inevitably face in business and in life. 'Grounded' captures your attention like few business books you've read before. You will learn principles of leadership that will help you survive and even thrive through the kinds of crises that befall every business. 'Grounded' is a must-read!"

— **Joe Calloway**
Hall of Fame Speaker and Best-Selling Author

"In 'Grounded, David Peterson has written a business book that is at once readable, relatable, and relevant. Quality guru W. Edwards Deming once said that experience, without theory, teaches nothing. David has shown that, armed with the 'grounded in' principles and with a company strategy that provides a testable hypothesis that frames the learning of a leader, experience can be an invaluable professor. He shares the lessons that he has learned in crisis leadership, both through his own experience and in studying the actions of others, in a way that will have you turning the pages just to see what happens next."

— **Dr. Jon Krispin**
Professor of Entrepreneurship,
Valdosta State University

"The 'Grounded' presentation kept us mesmerized and drove home a strong lesson of leadership and effective decision-making."

— **Jodi Moore**
Grounded Keynote Attendee

GROUNDED
"Anchor" Management for Strategic Leadership
and Effective Decision-Making

Hardcover ISBN   978-1-944340-02-5
Paperback ISBN   978-1-944340-00-1
eBook ISBN   978-1-944340-01-8

First Edition

Printed in the United States of America

GROUNDED

"Anchor" Management for Strategic Leadership and Effective Decision-Making

DAVID L. PETERSON

TABLE OF CONTENTS

FOREWORD

It has been an absolute pleasure and honor to know David Peterson for over thirty years. During that time, we have been co-workers, business partners, and industry leaders helping to shape the future of the Financial Services Industry.

David has always had a unique ability to grasp any situation and quickly visualize a path to success. Now, after reading this book, I have a better understanding of how he came to acquire those valuable skills—through real life experiences. Throughout *Grounded!*, David offers enlightening and thought-provoking strategies to improve anyone's leadership and decision-making skills. Whether you are a manager, business owner, or just aspiring to be in a leadership role, this book will help you.

Entrepreneurs, managers, and leaders of all types can agree that mitigating business disasters is a key objective. Having the forethought to make better decisions is a key strategy in that mitigation process. In Chapter 5, "Taking Corrective Action," I found the decision formula particularly valuable to use in a time of intense pressure to produce a positive outcome. We often avoid strategic decision fundamentals, get sidetracked by emotion or, worse yet, do nothing! This formula will help keep you on-course, so you don't steer too far off in any one direction.

Over the years, David and I have been in some very difficult business situations, and it was only by deploying business acumen in decision-making and staying grounded that we continually triumph. It wasn't until reading this book that I realized David has been exercising the skills he outlines in the following pages for many years. By working side by side with him, I was benefiting from those tactics without even realizing it. Now, you and everyone who has the opportunity to read the book will have the same advantage.

Grounded illustrates that acquiring "Grounded In" traits and minimizing "Grounded By" traits can make the difference between life and death in some situations, whether a business grows or dies, or perhaps whether a project gets launched. In reading *Grounded*, you will quickly see how the real life events discussed can be related to everyday operational decision processes.

Great leaders are never finished learning, and leadership is a constant journey. All of us need the challenge to review and renew our decision-making and leadership skills. *Grounded* is an exceptional leadership book that will help you become aware of the key characteristics found in effective and successful leaders.

Leaders are not always managers or business owners. They can be anyone with the capability and bravery to step forward in trying times and lead.

Weigh the anchor, hoist the sails, and enjoy the insight that is about to unfold as you sail the seas with David Peterson in *Grounded*.

— **Lori Frank**

Lori Frank is currently the President and CEO of Argos Risk, a company that specializes in web technology that manages credit risk. She has three decades of management experience within the financial services technology industry, including eight years of commercial banking and twenty years of "C" level management in technology companies. She has served as CEO of both private and public companies including INSCI Incorporated (INSI), ICU Data Systems, Imaging Institute/Towne Services. and DCR Technologies/Network Imaging. She has successfully co-founded and sold numerous technology companies over the years, providing attractive returns to the investors. Lori's expertise includes new product launches, market education, and product positioning. Her strong sales and marketing background has helped companies gain market share, enhance sales revenue, and achieve profitability.

INTRODUCTION

First of all, thank you for taking the time to read this book. It is my goal to make your investment pay off in usable wisdom and insight.

You may have received this book as a gift. You may have received it from a forward-thinking organization that hired me to give a keynote address and provide a book to every attendee. Maybe your manager gave you this book as part of your ongoing career development. Maybe you wound up owning the book in a white elephant gift exchange. Regardless of how it came to be in your possession, it is my honest desire that you take away important concepts to integrate into your business or personal life.

This book targets both managers and individuals. You might be a business owner, a CEO, or part of an executive management team. Or you might manage one or more people, but are not an executive. You might not be a manager at all. Maybe you work for yourself and you don't have any direct reports, but you still have to make decisions—opportunities to exhibit individual leadership. I've designed this book for you to gain insight, regardless of which level you're coming from.

If you are an individual, take the tips and insights I provide as personal enrichment. Use them to increase your value to the company you work for and use individual leadership to rise to new career heights. If you are a manager, supervisor, or business owner, and I am talking about management roles, I am speaking directly to you. When I am speaking to individuals about their managers, I am speaking about you. My hope is that you recognize yourself as a manager who is worthy of your direct reports' loyalty.

This book is written in a conversational style. I am using true sailing stories that highlight how leadership and decision-making exhibited in crisis scenarios are related to business and life. I am not, however, attempting to correlate the insights I espouse directly with formal terms of management concepts and techniques, though correlation is often visible nonetheless, as observed by friends who are experts in formal management systems such as Six Sigma. While I may reference these correlatives from time to time, the book is not steeped in formal management speak. If you are a Six Sigma Black Belt, I have the greatest respect for your achievements. Though this book is not written for you specifically, it is my hope that you will take away insights nonetheless.

This book focuses on three voyages that ended in disaster, three shipwrecks: the *Alacrity*, the *Grafton*, and the *Invercauld*, and how the anchors factored into their becoming *grounded*. I will share my personal story that occurred in the summer of 1979 when I was sailing the *Alacrity* with my dad, which ended in disaster. One hundred fifteen years earlier, an interesting event in maritime history occurred when the *Grafton* and the *Invercauld* both wrecked separately in the South Pacific on Auckland Island, with neither of the surviving crews knowing of the other's existence.

These two shipwrecks occurred on the same island, roughly five hundred kilometers south of New Zealand in bleak and desolate conditions. The way the two crews conducted themselves, and the manner in which they ultimately survived (or didn't), draws a stark contrast in the area of decision-making and leadership, especially considering the two captains. I dig further into what good leadership and decision-making looks like, especially in a time of crisis. You will learn what to do in advance to mitigate the negative impact of a crisis in business or life, even though crises are almost always unforeseen.

You may naturally ask, "If I don't know what the crisis will be, how can I prepare for it?" Through these shipwreck stories, my goal is to give you insight detailing how it is possible for you, in advance, to prepare information and resources that will lessen the impact of a crisis and avoid disaster.

This book is also about how leadership, effective decision-making, and overcoming adversity all come from being *grounded*. I will illustrate the key positive traits we need to accentuate and three negative traits we need to minimize. The proper imbalance of these traits—where the three positive anchors are strong, and the three negative anchors are limited—will allow people to not only remain calm, respond appropriately to difficult situations, and regard others before themselves, but also exhibit courage, show initiative, and persevere. Now, an anchor is an inanimate object. It can't do anything positively or negatively on its own. But in the hands of an actively thinking, grounded individual with the full knowledge of how to properly use it, it can be the instrument that prevents disaster.

In the back of the book, there is an appendix labeled *Digging Deeper*. There, you will find a short survey that will allow you to perform a self-evaluation of your "Grounded Quotient." This GQ test and my advice based on the results do not result from any specific knowledge of psychology or training I have. They are based on my observations, having worked with many hundreds of owners, managers, and workers at companies big and small.

Now strap yourself in. In the odd-numbered chapters, I'm going to take you on a journey to the Bahamas on the final voyage of the *Alacrity*. In the even-numbered chapters, we'll journey to Auckland Island in 1864 and examine the fate of the *Grafton* and the *Invercauld*, as well as the actions of the respective captains, Musgrave and Dalgarno. My goal is to weave these adventure stories into a narrative that allows you to understand what it means to be *Grounded*. Enjoy!

— David L. Peterson

PROLOGUE

This is how the end… began.

Whhumm.

At first, it was a barely perceptible vibration incorporated into my dream.

Whummm.

A bit more forceful, perhaps a bit out of place in my dream storyline.

Whump!

Now I was instantly awake, but not instantly aware. Where was I? The effects of thirty hours with little sleep had left me in a mental fog. I had forgotten the events of the previous day and a half.

WHUMP!

That jolted me back to the present. It was pitch black, but the rolling of the waves and the soft glow of the compass light quickly oriented me—our sailboat was off the coast of the Bahamas, and we were waiting for first light to enter the narrow harbor at West End.

WHUMP!

The sound and resulting vibrations were growing louder, more insistent. Then I heard breakers, waves cresting onto a beach. My heart stopped for an instant, and then began pounding in my chest. We must be drifting onto a reef!

WHUMP!

Then, in a rush, the following thoughts raced into my consciousness: we were offshore of the Grand Bahamas Bank. I was on watch. We are very close to a cay and —

WWHHUUMMPP!

The waves are pushing the sailboat onto the coral reef. We are about to be … Grounded!

CHAPTER ONE

Navigating the Crossing

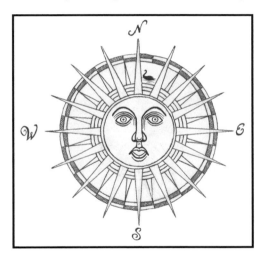

"When you have eliminated the impossible,
whatever remains, however improbable,
must be the truth."

— Sherlock Holmes

Summer 1979, 10:00 p.m. *Having loaded our sailboat, Alacrity,*
with provisions and made final preparations to sail, we untied her
from the dock and pushed off. On board were myself, my dad, and

my friend Vince. As the wind was light, we motored through the inter-coastal waterway toward the Palm Beach Inlet which opened to the Atlantic. It was late in the evening, which might seem an odd time to begin a sailing trip, but the timing was absolutely critical in a sailing vessel such as ours. Even though West End (aptly called, since it is on the western tip of the Great Bahama Island and the closest point to the US mainland from that island) was only seventy miles and a short powerboat ride away, our antique diesel engine took closer to ten hours to travel that distance.

The channel leading into the harbor at West End is quite narrow and, on either side of the channel, it is shallow—not just a bit shallow here and there, but only a couple of feet deep shallow everywhere. As our sailboat had nearly five feet of hull and keel below the waterline, we definitely needed to see where we were going! So, we always left the Florida coast in the dark, traveled through the night and arrived in the morning daylight. We had done this dozens of times over the past five years. Heading out of the Palm Beach Inlet, West End is virtually due east. However, we set a course slightly southeast, compensating for wind and current.

As per our usual routine, once we cleared the rocks protecting the inlet, we steered to 121 degrees on the compass. My dad and I took turns at the helm throughout the trip, with the bulkhead-mounted compass easily in sight. While we might vary a degree or two on either side of 121, it was fairly easy to keep the boat on course.

This trip had become routine for us and, over all those years, nothing unusual ever happened … until morning came. In the light of the new day, where we expected to see the familiar line of land against the horizon, we saw only water. 360 degrees of water. No land was in sight anywhere, with the open ocean stretching out in all directions.

Hyperawareness

If you're starting something new, embarking on something you've never done before, you are likely hypersensitive to the fact that everything about that process is a new experience. Say you decide to take up sailing. You have a general idea of the mechanisms that allow the sailboat to operate, you know that the sails catch the wind and move the boat forward and the wheel steers the boat, but you really don't know anything about sailing.

So, as you begin to sail or are taking sailing lessons, you focus on every aspect of how to sail, understanding why each element is important to eventual success. You ask a lot of how and why questions. You have to keep the sail in a specific position relative to the wind. Why? Oh, it makes a difference as to the direction and speed of the boat. Got it. Now, which line moves this sail? If you have been a sailor for twenty-five years, you would likely jump aboard any type of sailboat and instinctively figure out how it sails.

As a newbie sailor practicing out on the water, you can't anticipate everything that's going to happen. You're inexperienced, so as things first occur, you don't know whether or not this is something that happens in the normal course of sailing or if this might be something unusual. It just happens. You learn how to tack, moving the boat from one position of the sail to the wind and back again (yippee!), but the sailboat swings way past the correct sail position and you lose all the wind (crap!). Oh, the helm takes more time to react, and you have to slow down your turn before the sailboat has responded (learned behavior—success!). Once you experience a series of events in the same way over a period of time, a pattern is established of what is likely to occur over and over and over again. Only after repetition, over a period of time, do patterns of expectation become set, so you have an idea of how this activity normally goes.

The Numbing Effect of Routine

The correlative of being hyperaware of new things is the numbing effect of the routine. Regardless of whether you are a business leader or just a hardworking company staffer, the more acclimated you are to your job, the more likely you will be taken aback when something unexpected occurs. By definition, it's unexpected, so you cannot anticipate it. But if something unexpected occurred the first time you were doing a new activity, it wouldn't strike you as particularly unusual, nor would it likely have a dramatic negative effect because, in fact, you weren't expecting anything. You didn't know what was going to happen, and you were simply dealing with obstacles as they presented themselves.

A company with a routine procedure, however, is more likely to be negatively affected by the unforeseen event, simply because of the number of times it has methodically followed that procedure and not gone awry. Repetition breeds boredom, or at least a lack of vigilance. Repetition makes something coming out of the blue more likely to be negative, something improbable, like a Black Swan.[1]

1 Nassim Taleb wrote *The Black Swan*, which is focused on unexpected events in the financial markets. The main idea I learned from this book is that the Black Swan event, the unexpected event coming out of left field, is more likely to have a greater impact on an experienced individual or an organization repeatedly doing a certain process or procedure over a long period of time without a Black Swan event ever occurring. We get lulled into thinking, "This is how this works. This is what the process is." Therefore, we're much more taken aback if a Black Swan event happens after we've been doing something for a long time, like making the journey to the Bahamas. Whether one's response is to ignore the Black Swan altogether, or become paralyzed by it, it can exacerbate a situation into a serious problem.

I Just Don't Believe It

Prior to this particular trip in 1979, my dad and I had sailed together more than a hundred times.

David Peterson at 18 years old,
chillin' on *Alacrity,* circa 1979
—Laure Peterson Collection—

My dad was a trained educator; he had a doctorate in education and had risen from a schoolteacher to become a school administrator in New Jersey, and a college professor and administrator. As I was growing up, he was winding down his career by teaching thirteen- and fourteen-year-olds at a local private school.

Don Peterson, Schoolteacher
—Laure Peterson Collection—

Don Peterson, Mariner
—Laure Peterson Collection—

He hated to shave and had a full beard most of the time I was growing up. He used to keep it pretty long, something that I knew bugged my mom. As a teacher, he had long summer breaks and he spent that time sailing. He was so professional in the class and then, on the weekends or during the summer, he would always be wearing these ratty cutoff jeans with a rope belt. A rope belt! I am literally talking about a piece of line cast off the boat that he used in place of a belt with a buckle. With no shirt, old cutoff jean shorts, tan skin, a full head of salt and pepper hair, and this long beard, he looked every bit of a sailor. But within this rough-looking, old, and salty exterior were two of the most intelligent eyes I have ever seen. Never loud or brazen, he was quiet, thoughtful, and always encouraging, even when I made a mistake. I know so many people whose father was a terrible mentor and role model for them. I wish all of them could have known my dad as I knew him.

I began sailing with him when I was around eight years old in South Florida, a virtual playground for boating. The east coast of Florida provides great breezes with plenty of inlets to duck into if bad weather were to arise. And, the Intracoastal Waterway is a significant body of water that stretches the length of Florida. This sheltered and well-marked waterway is a great sailing venue in its own right. Regardless of whether you are offshore or inshore, you have great weather, even in the wintertime, and it's a great place to own a sailboat.

Separate from our local sailing waters, just seventy miles due east was Grand Bahama Island. Over the years, my dad and I had sailed to the Bahamas together dozens of times. We always left at about the same time at night, knowing generally how long the sailing journey would take. We knew exactly what the proper compass heading was. We always accounted for the wind and the currents. While the wind is not generally much of a factor at night, the Gulf Stream is literally a river of current, winding its way northward within the Atlantic Ocean, and it runs very close to the South

Florida coast. You have to account for its effect in planning for a destination that lies beyond its flow.

I still laugh today at our sailboat being named the *Alacrity*, which means "promptness in response." She was anything but.

She was a majestic boat, built when craftsmanship in wood and efficiency in design ruled the day. *Alacrity* was actually the fourth sailboat my dad had acquired. He started with a small Hobie Cat, the kind you can rent at most beach hotels. Next was a twenty-one-foot sloop, his first "real" sailboat. Aside from assisting him with maintenance and repairs of the boat, I remember painting the deck a beautiful pearly white that proved to be way too slippery when wet! That, of course, was a problem. My dad read that you could mix sand with paint to make a surface with good grip. Well, we lived about a hundred yards from the beach—acquiring sand was no problem. We had since run out of white paint, however, so my dad mixed the sand with a tar heel blue color paint he had in the garage. The sand worked great, but it was an awful color. Eventually he sold that boat and purchased a thirty-two foot ketch. We didn't have that boat very long, but it sailed great and we were extending our voyages farther from home, doing more and more overnight trips.

When the *Alacrity* caught my dad's eye, though it was in need of some TLC, it was love at first sight. And when my dad found out he could not yet afford the *Alacrity*, even after selling the thirty-two footer, he convinced a couple of other sailing buddies to go in with him. And soon, *Alacrity* was theirs.

I don't recall any scheduling conflicts to sail on the *Alacrity*—I wonder if those other guys ever even used her! After pulling her out of the water and spending an extended period of sanding, stripping, painting, and re-rigging, she was re-launched and immediately became the focus of Dad's available time and resources. She was big enough for more extended trips and we started making voyages to the Bahamas.

Mom and Dad at sail on *Alacrity*,
Don and Laure Peterson, circa 1979
—Laure Peterson Collection—

The *Alacrity*, a two-masted gaff-rigged schooner.
A beautiful and fun ship to sail … slowly.
—Laure Peterson Collection—

The *Alacrity* was slow to sail. If we left in the evening at 10 p.m., about ten hours later, as the sun came up, we would see the outline of land directly ahead. We might, perhaps, arrive a little to the south or a bit to the north of our destination, but whenever daylight came, we would be within a half mile of where we wanted to be, every single time.

Knowing that *Alacrity* was not a particularly fast boat, even in the best of conditions, we planned our departures for longer voyages carefully. On this particular trip in 1979, our expectations were the same. We would sail through the night on a specific compass heading, the sun would come up, and the Bahamas would be right there. But this time, as you know, the islands weren't right there. They were nowhere to be seen. We dropped the sails and just floated in the water. We couldn't believe the Bahamas were not there. Immediately, we assumed we had made an error. We must have used the wrong compass heading. But both my dad and I took turns at the helm, and we knew we were always one or two degrees from our time-honored setting of 121 degrees. We had followed the procedure perfectly. We had done every step correctly. We had executed each of the steps in their proper order and in the proper way, yet we didn't get the result we normally did.

If this had been our first or second crossing, I don't think we would have said something like, "Whoops! We must have our procedure wrong." We would have been curious, or maybe even concerned. But on this trip, we were dumbfounded. And we wound up wasting time thinking about how not seeing the Bahamas was impossible rather than working on identifying a solution. Wasted time cannot be recovered.

Beware Automated Thinking

So, how do we address this issue of becoming accustomed to how things work and succumbing to the numbing effect of repetition? Some companies have processes requiring someone to produce a sequenced set of steps, a form of human automation. They are hiring people to execute that process and not think for themselves. But, most businesses need people who can follow directions and also look for ways to improve their awareness to variances in the process. These companies must condition team members to constantly be vigilant of the possibility of what I call automated thinking.

Automated thinking is doing the next thing without thinking about what you're doing now. In organizations, automated thinking puts people into this robotic mode: "I pull this lever, then throw this switch and move this over to the other side and then turn this bar—and a good result occurs." Automated thinking puts your brain on autopilot, where the left side of your brain automatically knows what to do next and does so without giving it any thought.

Automated thinking can even prevent recognition of other external stimuli that might indicate, "Hey, something different is going on." The right side of your brain may be screaming for you to pay attention to something out of the ordinary. But the left brain is saying, "Nope! I'm doing B because that follows A, and then C follows B." You need to be cognizant of the fact that new stimuli, new information coming in, needs to be factored into the process, so you can decide whether or not C should follow B in this particular situation. Failure to recognize needed change will likely cause future problems. The more instances our automated expectations are met, the more susceptible we are to being shocked when we see a different result. It completely derails us from doing something immediately that could remediate the problem.

A Personal Black Swan

I founded Goldleaf Technologies in 1990 to produce software solving back-end operational issues in small to medium-sized community banks. By 2005, we had been writing software for fifteen years. Our approach had evolved time and time again as different platforms and technology became available and our end-users accessed the software through the public Internet or virtual private connections. We were using the latest and greatest development tools and had employees with multiple years of software experience. The management and senior leadership in the development area had all been long-time employees with highly evolved skills for developing software. We had comfortably settled into a pattern of software creation and deployment simply because our process worked.

You might assume that writing computer software wouldn't have the same process as a mechanical process; you'd use more of a thinking, analytical process. But, in some respects, the activities that go into software manufacturing are similar to assembly line manufacturing. People tend to follow the same patterns and do the same types of tasks repeatedly. For example, when you code something the same way every time, you expect the same results to occur in terms of the output of that coding. However, many times the code you're writing interacts with a lot of other pre-written code, and there may be multiple people writing the same application. You may have written a certain subroutine and used it many times, but now, all of a sudden, you're seeing a different result.

One of the Goldleaf systems that allowed financial institutions to create and initiate electronic transactions into the banking system had numerous iterations over the years, and the latest version had been actively running for four years. There were many hundreds of financial institution clients running it with tens of thousands of clients attached to all of those institutions. As with any software, there were always some bugs that caused the software to work in an unintended fashion.

Some of them were non-lethal, not particularly problematic. We jokingly referred to those as undocumented "features." For example, a word might wrap around on a report or something wouldn't line up correctly on the screen. Fairly benign. Then, there were bugs that caused the program to function improperly, but there was a way you could still make it work. Then, there were bugs that caused portions of the system to fail entirely without any work-around. In the world of software bugs, "undocumented features" are labeled Severity 3, bugs that have a work-around are Severity 2, and bugs that stop the show are Severity 1. When you have a Severity 1 bug, you have to stop everything and address that bug. You command all necessary resources to address the bug because there are serious repercussions.

The Death Spiral

The software in question was called ACH Client. This product was the primary tool by which businesses would interact with their financial institutions to send ACH debits and credits. I don't want to get into the details of ACH Client here, but suffice it to say this was a mission-critical application for the financial institutions and their business customers. If this product is not working, then they're not making payroll. They're not sending out debits to collect fees. They're not able to pay people for expense reimbursements, and on and on.

There were so many transactions. Millions of transactions were being created or processed through this ACH Client on a monthly basis through many hundreds of financial institutions. Every now and then, we hit a little bump in the road. Something would happen, a Severity 2 bug, and we would go in, figure it out, and fix it.

In 2005, on an ordinary Wednesday at three in the afternoon when everyone was minding their own business, numbingly moving proverbial levers, all of a sudden, the system started slowing down. Mind you, we didn't actually know it was slowing down. It was so intermittent and random, it didn't initially raise a blip on our internal monitoring systems. People started calling our support help desk about how slow the system was going. The system wasn't stopping or throwing any errors, it was sort of just grinding down to a halt, like a slow death spiral.

We started looking at the problem throughout that afternoon. We looked at some data that night and couldn't find anything that looked odd to us. The next morning, everything was fine. The system was operating within normal parameters. Everything looked good. Hmmm. It was a head scratcher. What was that about? What kind of blip was that? Then, it didn't happen the next day. Okay, it was just a glitch. Back to pulling levers and numbing routine. The day after that, Friday, it happened again. Hmmm, another glitch? But it didn't reoccur on the following Monday or Tuesday. Definitely a glitch. Then it occurred again on Wednesday. Now we have a serious problem. Apparently, three identical glitches over a week will register as a Black Swan in my left brain.

Over the following weeks, this death spiral would periodically occur. It wouldn't always happen on Wednesday, but frequently did so. When it happened, it was maddening. It would take a long time for the screens to return to the users for them to do their data entry. Anybody who was trying to use the system at that point was getting increasingly frustrated with how slow it was to access and use. To exacerbate the problem, most users would assume that something was wrong on their end, terminate the session, and start a new one. This artificially created more resource drain on the system because the old sessions were not releasing. (They actually were, but soooooo slowly.)

Because it was a "Software as a Service" (SAAS) system, it was affecting every user, every company, and every financial institution. Because of the overall slowdown, everyone who usually did their work earlier in the afternoon were still logged in when the late afternoon users logged in, only slowing the system further. The more logins, the slower the system functioned as it tried to manage all the resources. Of course, later in the day, people were trying to make five o' clock deadlines, which made the situation even worse as all these people rushed in to upload files or do their last-minute ACH transactions. We became more and more focused on what could possibly be going on.

What Are You Doing to Fix This?

We said, "Hey, this has to be a flaw in the software," so we checked for a software bug. We did everything we knew to do. We had all our people pouring through the code with a fine-tooth comb. We had our systems people looking at CPU cycles, memory, and disk utilization. We had network staff examining Internet connectivity. We tried to duplicate this anomaly in our test environment.

We couldn't duplicate it. We couldn't get it to do what it was doing in real life. Remember, this was not happening every day, but sporadically. Looking at every possible pattern that could occur still left us with no conclusions. As this intermittent death spiral continued over multiple weeks, I was on almost daily calls with senior management and hundreds of bank CEOs from our financial institutions. They all wanted to know, "What are you doing to fix this problem?"

There was no work-around. This was a Severity 1 bug, but it was a quandary because we couldn't identify where the problem originated. There were no errors being thrown. No discernible pattern. All these CEOs on the phone asked, "Why don't you switch over to your backup system?" But the backup system is merely a duplicate of the existing system; it's the same, identical code. There's nothing different in that code. This was not a situation that warranted the use of a backup system. They didn't understand; they just wanted it fixed and were losing their patience.

Here's the point: if we had recognized the original event as a Black Swan, instead of an insignificant glitch, we would have spent that week working on the problem and could have made significant progress in addressing the issue. Instead, we wasted time doing what we always did, what we automatically would do in this situation, and were, time and again, dumbfounded as to why we weren't achieving the desired result.

Identify the Black Swan Quickly (If You Can)

Understanding that a Black Swan event has occurred is paramount. It changes the focus of the response. If the ACH Client slowdown had occurred after we had just started development of the software, we probably would have looked at a number of different things, relative to all the components, instead of just assuming it had to be a particular bug in the code.

We had been running this system for four years and were responsible for so many customers and so many transactions. The volume was immense. We couldn't derive any pattern to any one customer or user. Suppose I only had ten customers on the system and nine of those customers had a few hundred transactions and one customer had hundreds of thousands of transactions that turned out to have hundreds of thousands of batches. That would be a much more stark contrast. "Hey! Maybe it's this one customer." When you're looking at log-ins, and you only have ten customers, you can see that every time the one customer logs in, things go awry.

Well, we did go look at who was logging in at those times, but there were thousands of people logged in. There was no way to isolate one particular customer amongst all the others. So much time had gone by and so many transactions had been made, this one particular user and this one particular setup didn't stick out as anything unique or unusual or anomalistic. It made the situation easier to hide.

Investigate All Improbabilities

Sometimes, you can't identify the problem, but you can identify what the symptoms are. Then, you work backwards. Ask questions like, "What are all the different kinds of elements or events that cause these symptoms?" I greatly admire Sir Arthur Conan Doyle, the physician and creator of Sherlock Holmes. You may have recognized the quote Doyle wrote, attributed to Holmes, at the heading of this chapter, "When you have eliminated the impossible, whatever remains, however improbable, must be the truth." We must specifically look for improbable things and eliminate them as suspects. We can't afford to say, "Well, that could never happen."

Make sure you've actually investigated all improbabilities and ensured they haven't happened. Never during all the weeks spent struggling with the mystery problem at Goldleaf did we ever engage in a process of determining everything it could possibly be, however improbable. In medicine, they call it a differential diagnosis. That is where a physician would determine the distinguishing characteristics of a particular disease or condition from others that present similar symptoms. If we had done this, particularly in the days after the problem first occurred, the idea that ultimately proved to be the solution would have surfaced as a possibility, and we might have saved weeks of unhappy customers and sleepless nights for our technical staff.

Whether you wake up to find that someone has moved the Bahamas or face a bizarre Black Swan situation within your organization, you've got to be prepared to quickly identify what the anomaly is and begin to work on a resolution. Set aside any possible startled reactions like, "Whoa, this can't be happening," and hyper-focus on all the different types of things it could be. See if something requires your immediate attention. Do you need to take some prompt action that remediates or lessens the problem right away? Is it likely that something you do might make the situation worse? Then quickly evaluate how you could utilize some outside stimuli.

CHAPTER TWO
The Two Shipwrecks

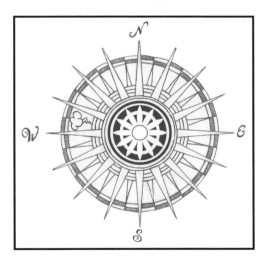

*"Live as brave men; and if fortune is adverse,
front its blows with brave hearts."*

— Marcus Tullius Cicero

Sometimes, the best way to illustrate the contrast between qualities such as good leadership and bad leadership or good decision-making and bad decision-making is to tell a story. Historical events, particularly disasters, provide a crucible for examining how individuals handle emergency situations. A perfect juxtaposition of positive and negative leadership and decision-making exists. It occurred one hundred fifteen years before the voyage of the *Alacrity* and involves the captains and crews of the *Grafton* and the *Invercauld*. Let me tell you their story.

On November 12, 1863, the sailing ship *Grafton* left Australia with five members on board, headed to Campbell Island where they were convinced they would find argentiferous tin ore (argentiferous meaning silver-bearing). If successful, this treasure hunt would make them all a lot of money. The crew consisted of Captain Thomas Musgrave, First Mate François Raynal, two seamen, George Harris and Alexander "Alick" McLaren, as well as a cook, Henry Forgès.

Crew of the Grafton, 1863
—University of Wellington, Victoria—

We know a great deal about this trip because multiple records of it have been written. Both Captain Musgrave and Raynal kept a journal of their adventures and mishaps. They documented their efforts to select a ship specific to their purposes, looking at many different vessels before settling on the *Grafton*. Captain Musgrave was cautious about choosing his crew, looking specifically for people who had solid seafaring skills. But for the critical hire of first mate, Musgrave knew that François Raynal had extensive experience as an engineer and as a gold prospector, having worked in the goldfields of Australia. Two benefactors funded the trip: Musgrave's uncle and his uncle's business partner in Australia, Charles Sarpy. Before they left, Raynal insisted that the benefactors agree to alert the government to arrange for a rescue if the ship did not return in four months.

The *Grafton* Wrecks

They sailed to Campbell Island on November 12, 1863, arriving after a journey of ten days, and over the next six weeks thoroughly searched the island. They found no evidence of the silver-bearing ore. It's not surprising, because there was ample evidence that Campbell Island would not be a good place to find this ore, something that Musgrave and Raynal ignored. They should have known better, but both men were blinded by fortune. After coming up empty-handed on Campbell Island, they sailed to Auckland Island on December 29, hoping to get enough seal skins to make the trip worthwhile.

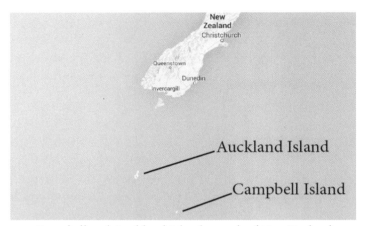

Campbell and Auckland Islands, south of New Zealand
—Google Maps—

On January 3, 1864, a terrific storm pushed the ship close to the rocky coast and the crew was unable to keep the *Grafton* from wrecking. Using the dinghy, they were able to go ashore and transfer some goods from the ship onto the beach the following day. Auckland Island is a desolate place, about 500 kilometers south of New Zealand. In the summer (November to February), swarms of biting flies cover the islands, and the winters (May to August) are brutal with snow, sleet, and harsh winds. Over a decade prior, a group had attempted to settle on the island, but it failed after three years. For the castaways, finding food and building a shelter was imperative.

They had a few advantages. The *Grafton* was nearby and accessible at low tide. They couldn't just swim out to it, but they had the dinghy and were able to start harvesting additional resources. Raynal was able to find his gun and some ammunition. They were able to collect wood, tools, and iron from the ship, which remarkably never sank or broke apart while the men were stranded on the island.

For a month, they spent their time finding sources of food and building a sturdy shelter. Growing a garden was futile, but they discovered ways to kill and cook seal and sea lion meat. They were able to shoot and cook some birds. They eventually discovered the edible Stilbocarpa polaris, a mega-herb that offered carbohydrates, vitamins, and fiber. They finished building a cabin that would protect them for the long months ahead.

Grafton initial shelter
—Alfred De Neuville Engraving, Public Domain—

A cabin to shield them from the wind and biting flies
—Alfred De Neuville Engraving, Public Domain—

Democracy on Land

It became clear that the normal separation of officers and seamen that exists on sailing ships was no longer workable for this stranded crew. Although Musgrave believed that the captain should have absolute authority over the crew, since the shipwreck, he had worked side by side with these men, sharing the resources and the workload.

The men began to resent feeling inferior and wanted a true democratic process instated for leadership. Raynal suggested a solution to the brewing animosity: they would vote for a leader—not a dictator, but a chief to keep things orderly and assign tasks. The seamen added a clause that allowed the chief to be fired and replaced if he led poorly. All five survivors agreed to this. Raynal nominated Musgrave, who was unanimously voted as their chief.

In the horribly long months to come, Musgrave was never fired. The fact that he agreed to the voting process and acknowledged their equality showed his wisdom. Even though he periodically suffered from bouts of depression, especially worrying about his wife and children alone in Sydney, he consistently kept the survivors together and made decisions that saved their lives on multiple occasions.

One of the most amazing things to me about this story is that, after they were more settled, Captain Musgrave instituted nightly education classes, so they could train each other in their various areas of expertise. Since Raynal was a Frenchman, he taught them how to speak French. Alick had some math skills, so he taught algebra. Each of them shared a level of expertise from his own unique set of skills. Why did they take the time to do that?

Musgrave leads the survivors in nightly education classes
—Alfred De Neuville Engraving, Public Domain—

Musgrave knew if they had purpose, a reason for existing and pushing forward, they would be mentally engaged and less likely to despair. Keeping busy with tasks and either preparing to teach or going to class kept their minds active. It also gave them less time at night to dwell on how dire their situation truly was.

Another habit Musgrave established early on was Bible readings after dinner. What an amazing amount of leadership Captain Musgrave showed in terms of keeping them all together! His wisdom, along with Raynal's constant support and counsel, conditioned the group for survival. They had few arguments and began to truly care for each other.

Rescuing Themselves

They established a routine and waited for October when a rescue ship was supposed to come, according to the timetable that Raynal had established with Charles Sarpy. They put up a signal flag. They created a big bonfire and had fire always available to light the blaze at a moment's notice. They were regularly scanning the sea, setting a watch at the highest point of the hill above their hut.

The time came and went when they expected a rescue ship. And then more months went by. Then more months went by—months of deprivation, cold, injuries, and cycles of despair and hope again. Almost a full year passed.

On Christmas Day, 1864, they were not doing well. Sadness was overtaking all of them. However, Raynal, in a burst of hope, told the men they must try and build another boat from scratch and save themselves.

Raynal had the ingenuity and engineering skill to build a forge. A working forge in the middle of this desolate, foreboding place! Raynal started crafting tools and nails using iron salvaged from the *Grafton*. At one point, they had to abandon the boat building because there was one tool Raynal just could not figure out how to make.

Again, despair began to take over. They had been so close. They had to do something! They were at the point of saying, "Look, we're either going to stay here and die, or we can all make the attempt in the dinghy."

Raynal's ability to make tools was critical
to their survival and self-rescue.
—Alfred De Neuville Engraving, Public Domain—

After discussing their options, they decided to strengthen the dinghy and sail her to the closest landmass, which was New Zealand. Still using the forge and the tools Raynal had already made, they worked day and night to augment the little craft into a boat that could safely transport them in the open ocean. An amazing amount of workmanship went into the re-making of this dinghy. It took them months of back-breaking labor, but they finally got it done.

Grafton crew working on making the dinghy seaworthy
—Alfred De Neuville Engraving, Public Domain—

They tested it, sailing it around a little part of the island with all five castaways aboard. Musgrave realized immediately there was no way for all five of them to survive the trek in this boat all the way to New Zealand. He decided he could only take two men with him, and two men would have to stay. All of them wanted to stay together. No one wanted to die of starvation on the island, and no one wanted to drown in the sea. Musgrave finally decided that Forgès the cook, who, after the short trip in the boat, decided he didn't want any part of it, and the seaman, George Harris, who got along well with Forgès, would stay behind.

When all was ready, Raynal, Alick, and Musgrave set off in the boat. After five frightful days at sea and multiple life-threatening events, they did in fact arrive at a safe harbor at Invercargill, New Zealand. They were treated well and taken to a port city, where they convinced authorities to organize a rescue mission for the other two castaways. Musgrave, who desperately wanted to return to Sydney to check on his family, joined the crew, sailed back to Auckland Island, rescued his two crew members, and searched diligently all over the island to make sure no other castaways would be left behind to suffer what he had suffered.

A total capsize — just one of the terrors
in sailing the dinghy back to New Zealand
—Alfred De Neuville Engraving, Public Domain—

Clear Leadership

From the very beginning of their horrific time on the island, there was never a time recorded that Captain Musgrave didn't strategically think through all the different options available to him, weigh the risks and the rewards, and consistently make decisions that factored in the welfare of his fellow castaways.

He had chosen, in Raynal, somebody who had an eclectic skill set. For example, Raynal made soap, which turned out to be a huge blessing for five people who were living in a very small, cramped space. Raynal crafted shoes out of seal skins and made concrete from crushed shells. Raynal's ingenuity went far beyond any skills he needed to look for the argentiferous tin or to collect seals. Having that type of resource was clearly a huge plus for the *Grafton* crew.

Raynal making shoes from sealskins
—Alfred De Neuville Engraving, Public Domain—

At the end of the day, though, their survival came down to Captain Musgrave and his ability to think clearly in a time of crisis, to make good decisions, and to consider the welfare of the entire enterprise, especially the men who were entrusted to his care. His exhibition of calm focus, thoughtful action, and regard for others clearly illustrate a grounded captain, capable of strategic leadership and effective decision-making.

Now, let's contrast this with the captain of another ship, which met a fateful end on Auckland Island in 1864: Captain Dalgarno of the *Invercauld*.

The Wreck of the *Invercauld*

Amazingly, only eighteen miles away from where the *Grafton* survivors were eking out an existence, the 188-ton, square-rigged *Invercauld* wrecked on the far north end of Auckland Island on July 10, 1864. We don't have detailed information about the preparations that went into the *Invercauld's* expedition, such as we have with the *Grafton*, but we do know a few things.

For one, the ship's hold was empty. The *Invercauld* was on its way to South America to pick up a load of fertilizer, so the ship was very light, riding too high in the water, which is a dangerous situation for a sailing ship. The more ballast there is in the hold, the more settled the ship rests in the water and the more stable it is as a vessel.

The captain had posted watches to make sure they would see land as they neared the area. So, when one of the watches yelled, "Land ho!" Dalgarno, falsely assuming they were at the southwestern end of Adam's Island, decided to fall off on a starboard tack which would take him around the island.

Shipwrecks
- Derry Castle (1887)
- Invercauld (1864)
- Dundonald (1907)
- General Grant (1866)
- Anjou (1905)
- Grafton (1864)

Location of the Grafton and Invercauld wrecks.
(Note the volcanic terrain.)
—Encyclopedia of New Zealand—

The Jaws of Hell

Of course, he was not where he thought he was at all. He wound up sailing into what was later called "The Jaws of Hell," one of the most dangerous stretches between two parts of Auckland Island. Dalgarno was confused when, after a short time, more land was sighted.

In his confusion, he tried to get the sail to luff into the wind, meaning it would point straight into the wind, causing the boat to stall forward motion, so he could take stock. Instead, the ship fell away from the wind. In doing so, it lost its maneuverability and was doomed.

The ship wrecked horrifically on the jagged rocks and six men instantly perished. Nineteen survivors made it to a small horse-shoe-shaped, desolate beach with a three-hundred-foot cliff of sheer rock above them. It was snowing and sleeting, and the wind blew with a fury. Few resources from their ship washed ashore: about two pounds of soaked biscuits and two pounds of salt pork. Only the stern of the *Invercauld* could be seen, and they had no access to it whatsoever. Within just a few days, it sank completely.

Wrecked with limited resources
—Alfred De Neuville Engraving, Public Domain—

A Leader Emerges

From the start, Captain Dalgarno, First Mate Andrew Smith, and Second Mate James Mahoney, never offered any meaningful leadership. Dalgarno couldn't believe his ship was wrecked and was seemingly incapacitated. He did not take charge. He did not organize his men. He never said anything like, "Okay, here's our survival plan. You men go climb this three-hundred-foot precipice and figure out where we can get off this tiny beach. You men go look for food." He did nothing. All three officers went into numb mode.

A couple of men climbed up to look around, returned, and said, "Hey, we saw sheep tracks." One sailor, Robert Holding, who had also been a prospector in the goldfields of Australia, and observing the void in leadership, decided to exhibit individual leadership. He climbed up the rock face and figured out the tracks were not from sheep, but pigs. He came back down and organized the process of moving everyone off the beach.

He knew they had to get off that beach. There were no seals in the area and there were few Stilbocarpa plants nestled in the cracks of the rocks. They didn't have the resources to sustain a couple of men, much less nineteen; they had to reach the plateau. So, he organized them and coerced them to start climbing. Once on the plateau, some of the men started to explore on their own, but some of them didn't come back. They lost people. Four of them went to hunt the pig and only three of them came back. They reported that the other sailor just lay down in the grass and wouldn't move.

The group started to fracture quickly, and Holding was the one trying to keep them together. He prevented them from hurting themselves or doing stupid things.

For example, they discovered they had two boxes of matches. Now, as you can imagine, a box of matches is a precious commodity in their situation. They could light a fire, cook, and stay warm. They lit a fire during the first night, and the ship's cook, in an attempt to dry off the rest of his matches, wound up setting the entire box on fire. Whoosh! They were all gone. Then the first mate attempted to do the same thing with the second box, but Holding snatched the matches from him and refused to give them back. Although he was a common seaman, he was the only person clearly thinking from a survival standpoint.

Leadership Fail

The captain and first mate were regularly ordering the crew around. "Go get me water." "Go get me food." They were still acting like they did on the ship, with a dictatorial authority over the crew who were at their beck and call. They continued to exhibit no leadership, no decision-making, letting the men act and behave at will.

Holding was the one who truly thought through their options. He constantly exhibited individual leadership. After getting the crew up to the plateau, he couldn't convince them to move to a place with more resources. Some of them were literally sitting down in the grass saying, "We're not moving. We're done."

Now, lest we place all of the blame for the fate of the sixteen men who died on Auckland Island on Captain Dalgarno, Robert Holding himself offered insight into additional factors that lessened their chances. From his personal journal, Holding said this of the *Invercauld* crew: "It is probable that had we been better acquainted with each other things might have been somewhat different." The crew didn't even know each other's names, so there was no camaraderie to bring them together with a common purpose. We'll revisit this point later as we discuss the importance of the collective vibe amongst employees.

Survival

Eventually, there was talk of cannibalism. This disgusted Holding and he decided, in order to survive, he needed to part ways with the group. He found an abandoned encampment, which was the result of the previously mentioned failed attempt to colonize Auckland Island in the 1850s. He returned to the group still lying about the plateau to persuade them to come to this more sheltered place. Only three came with Holding to the abandoned town, including Dalgarno and Smith.

During the following months, Holding continued to search for food; he figured out how to catch birds and kill seals. He reasoned that this encampment was the place to which potential rescuers would come, so they stayed in that area for a significant amount of time while the resources held out.

Killing seals was initially easy,
as they had no fear of people
—Alfred De Neuville Engraving, Public Domain—

The three eventually moved to other locations in search of better food sources. At no time did they have any knowledge whatsoever of the *Grafton* five who were a mere eighteen miles away on the other side of the island. The topography would not have allowed them to reach the other side, anyway. There was no beach to walk around, only impassable forests, steep mountains, and deep crevasses.

A Negative Example of Being Grounded

Captain Dalgarno's actions on Auckland Island are representative of traits of a different type of grounded, stuck in place with no drive, no initiative, and no leadership. He was selfish, passive, and exhibited no thoughtful action of any kind. He made poor decisions and did not exhibit any strategic behavior toward his men's survival. Yet, in spite of Dalgarno's lack of leadership, he, Smith, and Holding were ultimately rescued. They had moved to a different part of the island seeking new food sources and happened to be in the right place at the right time when they sighted a ship off the Auckland coast.

The sailing vessel *Julian*, on its way to South America, was seeking a safe harbor for repairs and happened to sail within their view. Holding lit a signal fire to attract attention and the three *Invercauld* survivors were overjoyed to see the boat lowered. When the three finally made it onboard the Julian, they were received well and offered new clothes. But when it was time to leave, the *Julian* never explored the rest of Auckland Island. They never sailed around the other side of the island where the *Grafton* crew was so desperate for rescue.[2]

---

2 For further details on these shipwrecks, read *Island of the Lost: Shipwrecked at the Edge of the World* by Joan Druett. I used her book as a resource for *Grounded*.

CHAPTER THREE

Reassessing Our Position

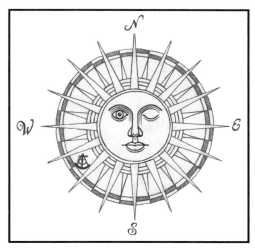

"Where the senses fail us, reason must step in."

— Galileo Galilei

Seeing only water where we expected to see land was unsettling, disturbing. Where in the heck were the Bahamas? Where were we? Completely taken off guard, my dad retrieved the sextant from the cabin and took a sighting. This was before the era of global positioning satellites. Now, even a child can use a smartphone to find out exactly where he is. We had the compass, nautical charts, and the sextant.

After some sightings, some calculations, and then more sightings, my dad determined that, for some unknown reason, we had sailed far south of our target. Using the results of the sextant, he affixed our position on a nautical chart. We were southwest of West End, Bahamas. I had no reason to doubt him. He was an experienced sailor, and his experience dwarfed mine. He had used a sextant successfully many times. He was confident of his calculations. Subsequently, we felt confident we would now get back on track and be in the warm waters of the northern Bahamas within a few hours.

As I discussed in Chapter 1, repeating certain processes or procedures many, many times tends to make you immune to the realization that something other than the intended result could occur. Another way to examine a Black Swan event has to do with the urgency required to resolve it. Some things have to be dealt with immediately because you are in imminent danger.

If you are walking through the woods and step into a clearing, and on the other end of the clearing is a mother bear and two cubs, you have to make some quick decisions. You don't have time to get out your laptop and look up what to do when you encounter a bear. You don't have time to call somebody on the phone and say, "Hey! What do you know about the right way to escape an encounter with a bear?" If you immediately assess the situation and determine the bear hasn't noticed you, it may be possible to silently, without turning your back, slowly back out of that clearing and go around another way. That's the proper course of action in that scenario. It would be totally stupid to say loudly, "Oh, great. A bear. That's all I need!" Now the bear is aware of your presence, and your options are now severely diminished or eliminated, including the option of you quietly backing out of the clearing.

Maintain a mindset that prevents a Black Swan event from taking you out of rational thinking, so you can quickly assess a potentially dangerous situation and take immediate action, leading to a positive result.[3]

Missing the Window of Opportunity

How would this play out in a business scenario? Say you were manufacturing a product, and you shipped to your customers through the United States Postal Service (USPS). On a particular day, the shipping clerk didn't do his job, and the USPS came and went and didn't pick up these packages because they did not have the proper postage affixed to them. A bonehead, silly example. But it happens. You are hopping mad that these packages didn't go out, and you go a little crazy, verbally thrashing this individual who didn't get the postage right. You just lost the opportunity for immediate action. If the USPS carrier is gone, but you still need to ship those boxes, you have other options. Have the employee drive the packages to the post office. Beyond that there are UPS, FedEx, or any number of different carriers. You could drive the packages to the airport, ship them by air, and have them picked up at the destination.

Those options require you to quickly assess the situation. Ask yourself, "Is it critical for me to get these packages delivered today?" Answer that question. If the answer is no, then you've got more time. If the answer is yes, then ask Question #2, "What is the next quickest option that's most economical for me?" So, instead of wasting time verbally thrashing somebody about not properly using USPS, you need to be in contact with UPS or FedEx so you don't miss the shipping window. I realize this is a simple example, but people waste time on thoughts and behaviors that will not lead

---

3 The bear example is not a true Black Swan event. I mean, if you are walking in the woods, it's entirely possible you would encounter a bear. Now, if a meteor was hurtling its way to the clearing, that would be more Black Swan-like. However, I was struggling to figure out how quietly backing out of a clearing with a meteor about to wipe out a square mile around the clearing would make any sense. Maybe the meteor is small, like a baseball, like "Oh hey, there's a cute little meteor coming into the clearing. I think I'll just quietly back out...."

to a positive result and miss other opportunities that could have been viable options to resolve that problem.

If I Act Quickly Enough

Contrasted with the emergency Black Swan is a situation where you have the luxury of time to respond to what has occurred. Wasting time is never recommended, but in this scenario you are not at grave risk by delaying action. In most business situations, you don't find yourself in the equivalent of walking into a clearing and seeing a bear.

If you're faced with a situation that leads you to think it is atypical, then ask yourself, "Is this is a Black Swan event—something unlikely to occur, but with potentially negative, even catastrophic consequences for my business?"

If so, then ask, "Do I have to take immediate action, or do I have some time available to gather more information? How much time do I have given the potential severity of the situation and the speed with which it is unfolding?"

Consider the following chart of your actions based on emergency or non-emergency situations:

	Shock/ Surprise	Keep Your Head
Emergency – Requires immediate decisions	Big trouble – You are likely to make things worse.	Think quickly and act quickly. You have time to back out of the clearing.
Non-Emergency – You have time	Wasting time – May not hurt you in the long run, but it has no value to resolving the problem.	If you have the time, take it. Think through multiple courses of action and reach out to others who might be able to offer suggestions or meaningful information.

Keeping your head about you is the method most likely to yield positive results in all scenarios. Easy to say, hard to do. It takes practice and the mental fortitude to be ready to keep your head without prior warning of the need to do just that.

How We Got Here Isn't Important Right Now

Consider my situation with the *Alacrity*. We made this Bahamas trip dozens of times and only this one time was different. I realize this is crazy and irrational, but my first thought was, "The Bahamas aren't where they're supposed to be." We followed the correct compass heading. We did everything right. We were where we were supposed to be. Where are the Bahamas?

Being out on the water with no land in sight is both amazing and a bit discomforting. Amazing, as in the complete absence of any civilization. With the exception of the occasional airplane 25,000 feet up and perhaps seeing large ships well off in the distance, you are truly alone with nature. Things that you don't pay much mind to on land all of the sudden take on a new importance to your senses. The wind is a critical component of forward momentum on a sailboat. And it carries the sweetness of the salt air. The coolness of the breeze at night provides a refreshing way to sleep out on deck. The deeper water is a rich, dark blue and provides a contrast to the azure blue of the sky. You will see birds now and then, and the creatures of the sea will periodically make their presence known: dolphin, flying fish, and rays. I have even seen a whale in the Atlantic Ocean. Once in open water, we encountered a sunfish, one of the truly bizarre fish in the sea. But these are fleeting moments. Because, simply, it's a really big ocean, about forty-one million square miles for the Atlantic, and you are on a small boat, covering an infinitesimal fraction of that space.

So, the open ocean can make you a little crazy. Everything can look the same, in every direction, with no reference point on the horizon. Thus, as we were occupying a place in the Atlantic where the Bahamas were supposed to be, a crazy idea popped in my head that, somehow, something wrenched the islands out and shifted them a couple hundred miles, just to play with our minds a little bit.

Now, in this particular situation, we were out in the middle of the ocean, no land in sight. But, it was a nice morning all in all, a cloudless or nearly cloudless day. There were no signs of danger. There was no ship bearing down on us. There was no ginormous squid coming up to swallow our boat. We were just lazily hanging out in the water. This was not an "emergency" Black Swan. We had the luxury of time to try and determine what happened.

To my dad's credit, he didn't waste a lot of time trying to determine what had put us in this spot. He asked once if I had stayed on compass heading 121 but never accused me by saying, "What compass heading did you steer to again? You put us off course!" The most important thing we needed to know at that moment was exactly where we were. How we got to that spot was completely unimportant in the context of solving this problem. Remember, this was pre-GPS, pre-satellite phone, pre-anything that would have given us an immediate and fixed position, tracking through the satellites. We had a chart and our heading and speed that told us we should be at West End. We were obviously somewhere different from where we should have been. So, if we are not where we think we're supposed to be, where are we?

Where Are We Anyway?

This question of "Where are we?" is critical. Out in the middle of the ocean, with no indication of our position other than the movement of the sun, we had no idea in which direction to move.

We had a compass which gave us direction, but, as we'll see later in the story, it may have been the compass itself that was not operating correctly, which led us to this unintended location. Knowing where you are and being able to take immediate stock of your exact location is essential. Unless there is a dangerous situation, something that immediately has to happen because waiting causes you to lose options, then take the time to figure out exactly where you are.

My dad was able to fix our position on the chart in a different place than we anticipated we would be. Now, we could put an "X" on that chart and say, "We are here." What's the big deal about that? Why is it so critically important? Well, if we know our destination—West End, Bahamas—and we know where we are, now it's possible to set a new course that will take us in that specific direction.

At this point, you might legitimately say, "Hey David, if your compass was kinda wonky, doesn't that mean you could be heading off in the wrong direction again?" That's true. But, we now had the luxury of daylight, which allowed us to fix our position relative to the sun to make sure we were, in fact, moving in the right direction. Even though we didn't necessarily know that it was n degrees heading based on where the new position on the map said we were, we knew we had to move in a northeasterly direction if we wanted to get to West End based on our position fix from the sextant.

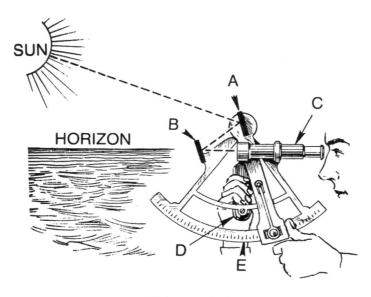

Using a sextant.
If it looks complicated, that's because it is.
—Public Domain—

Build a Road Map

How does this translate to a business environment? When an anomaly has occurred, you need to quickly ascertain all the important environmental issues. Gather whatever might be necessary—whatever data reference points, whatever information—for you to confirm exactly where you are, the proverbial "we are here," and to place an "X" on the map. If you have a software problem blow up, you want to get all the information from error logs, any information that would help identify what specifically is happening with the software. You assign experts to look at all the parts of the system where errors are being thrown that give clues to what the source of the problem is.

There are, however, unique metrics for your business that allow you to set an important stake in the ground as a way of saying, "We are here." In fact, as these events happen, you'll notice these same types of data points are the critical ones over and over again, guiding you to a solution. As you encounter these, you should create a matrix, almost a questionnaire, for yourself that says, "When an event happens, this is what I know."

Immediately, you can say, "Okay, Joe, you determine this and this. Sally, grab this information. Bill, you're going to find this and this." If everyone knows there's a procedure for obtaining certain information to ascertain where you are, that pushes immediate activity toward making that assessment. It puts people in the mode of data acquisition and problem solving, not standing around pointing fingers and trying to figure out who is at fault. That in and of itself is a good, positive change. If you can develop the idea of having a checklist to quickly confirm your position, you will already have a plan in place if an event were to occur. There may be some variations on that plan, some differences between the information you have to get for this situation and that situation. That's okay. You can build and augment your "Here's Where We Are" roadmap template every single time an event occurs.

Move Forward with the Best Information You Have

Having the knowledge of exactly where you are gives you the ability to make more intelligent decisions relative to possible courses of action. Using my Goldleaf slowdown example, if all the evidence pointed to a coding problem, an actual bug, and we could trace it exclusively to something happening in the code, then it would be reasonable to expect programmers to resolve that. If, on the other hand, all the "Here's Where We Are" evidence was pointing to an issue with the database, then it makes more sense to have database analysts looking at the situation rather than coders.

As I've already shared, sometimes it's none of those things. But from a known position, you make decisions to move in a direction that points toward a successful conclusion. Until you have evidence that the direction you're going isn't correct, there isn't much sense in altering course. That is not to say you shouldn't still consider any available sources that might provide updated information.

Returning to my story of the *Alacrity*, we knew we needed to move in a north and easterly direction. So, we raised our sails and headed out on that new course. There was no reason to continue going southeast or go more south or head due north. The only potential purpose for going back west would have been to actually return home the way we came. All these other possibilities are courses of action we could have taken, but, based on the assessment of where we were and the knowledge of where West End was, according to the chart (assuming somebody hadn't picked up the Bahamas and moved them!), heading northeast was the logical direction.

What other variables were there? Well, we could have run under motor, which would take us northeast at a certain speed. We could run under sail, which, depending on the wind, would have taken us at a different speed (potentially quicker than the engine, but most likely slower). Plus, the wind direction may not allow us to sail directly northeast. So, how fast I want to reach my destination is an issue. There was a limited amount of diesel fuel on board and, although the diesel engine used fuel slowly, we had to think about whether we wanted to use up all of our diesel fuel in order to make this new course or not. There was the unknown of when we would be able to obtain more fuel.

Allocating Resources

So, as you make your course correction, there are some important sub-decisions to think about relative to how you're best utilizing available resources. If I have twenty-five people in a software development shop, do I assign all of them to a particular problem? No. I create smaller teams to chase down the contributions of multiple potential root causes. The initial response is a divergent response—what are all the possible root causes/potential special circumstances that might cause the symptoms we are observing?

In the Goldleaf example, we might start at an even higher level of analysis. What are all of the potential categories of causes? Software? Hardware? Internet bandwidth? User volume (singular or cumulative)? Virus/Malware? Then, using these broad categories, one can drill down and begin to identify more specific causes, followed finally by the convergent process of considering and narrowing the list of actual contributors to the issue by process of elimination. When we come up with a rational course of action, the equivalent of heading northeast, I might have three people who continue to work on a specific solution, and I would turn the other twenty-two people loose to go back to working on other things.

At some point, you have to think about the appropriate use of resources. At the beginning of the crisis, you may have an all-hands-on-deck approach toward solving the problem, but then you decide on an appropriate number of resources to address it. Any more than that would not necessarily be productive based on the expected course of action you're taking to resolve the problem.

Knowing When to Change Course

Over time, I have found the best course of action is to rationally think through the issue, figure out where I am, come up with a course of action, and then utilize reasonable resources to go after that solution. At the very moment I feel like that course is no longer fruitful, I want to stop, take a new assessment and move in another direction.

Although he ultimately did wreck the *Invercauld*, Captain Dalgarno realized that he was not where he thought he was and stopped his forward motion on that fateful night in the summer of 1864.

In other words, I'm not going to waste time going down a path just because my gut reaction says it's the right one. Having said that, only in the face of clear evidence can I determine that an option is not working. For example, suppose while traveling on the *Alac-*

rity, we looked at the map and determined that, at best, sailing in a northeasterly direction at five knots would take five hours to get to West End. After two hours we say, "We don't see West End yet, so this is clearly not working." This is not rational. We already know from our own calculations it should take at least five hours in order to get to the island. So, you have to make sure you don't give up too quickly as you work on a resolution. When you don't have enough time to do it again, take the time to do it right the first time.

I've seen a lot of businesses do this. They choose a course of action, and after a period of time, whether that is a few days, weeks, or months, the desired result is not happening. Should the desired result have happened within that time frame? If it logically should take longer—if you quit on something after a few days that should take a few weeks—you're not allowing time for the solution to evolve.

At the same time you're taking stock and listening to your gut feeling about what you're going to do about the crisis, you also need to have some reasonable expectation about how long it should take for a resolution to manifest itself, or how much time should pass before you see positive evidence that a resolution is in sight. Only until that amount of time has been spent, or unless there's overwhelming new evidence coming in that tells you that you're doing something wrong, should you change course.

Suppose it was still dark at night, and we had decided to make a course correction on the *Alacrity* to go northeast. Suppose we did that for an hour, and then the sun came up and we could tell from the position of the sun in the east that we weren't going northeast, but going almost completely north. That's new information. Even though it hasn't been the five hours we know it will take us, we now have new evidence that tells us we're going in the wrong direction. Because we had gone a certain distance in the wrong direction, we wouldn't just automatically go northeast. At that point, we would have to stop, get the sextant out, and reestablish our position on the map.

Just as in sailing, it's critically important for you to know where you are so you can set the correct course to get where you need to go. As you move down the path of resolution, you're changing some of the variables. Those changed variables may have an impact in terms of what you need to do now in order to affect resolution.

Understand that getting a fix on your exact position, whether in sailing or in business, is the most critical thing to know before you make a decision about what to do next.

CHAPTER FOUR

The Two Captains

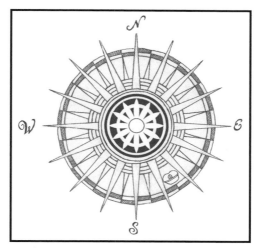

*"Each man is questioned by life: and he can
only answer to life by answering for his own life;
to life he can only respond by being responsible."*

— Viktor Frankl

Perhaps there was nothing that could be done to avoid the shipwrecks of the *Grafton* and the *Invercauld* on Auckland Island in 1864. However, I want to focus on the leadership and decision-making of the two captains. We could potentially question both of their decision-making skills regarding why they wrecked in the first place. Even in 1864, captains had rudimentary charts; they had access to information about the waters in which they were sailing. This was not the first time anyone had ever sailed to Auckland Island.

Limited Information

They had maps, but nothing on those maps told them about the depth of the water, the currents, what the weather would be, how the winds would be blowing from a certain direction, and so on. They also didn't have any motors, so, once they went into a particular area, the only way for them to leave would be for the wind to change or perhaps for the crew to row the ship out with dinghies. In many sailing stories from this time, you find a ship was stalled in one place for months waiting for the winds to change.

There was no satellite data, no GPS device you could hold in your hand with access to detailed charts. The only effective way to tell the depth of the water was with a lead line, a string or rope with a lead sinker and markings on it every fathom (six feet). A crew member would drop this in the water, typically from the bow of the boat, and call out how many fathoms until the weight hit the bottom of the sea. "Three fathoms." Okay, the water's eighteen feet deep. Only by doing that would they have an idea about whether the water was getting deeper or shallower or what the conditions were.

They had some information about the islands but, unlike today, had no equivalent to the National Oceanographic and Atmospheric Administration (NOAA), which provides detailed charts with depths in either feet or meters and highlights key areas for sailors. Today, we can go online and access tide schedules and know, "Today, at 1:00 in the afternoon, low tide will be 1.8 feet below normal." A modern-day sailor would then know that the water depth, which is normally five feet, will today be 3.2 feet at 1:00 p.m.

Still, around sailing ports of that time, information about destinations was widely shared, and it is likely that both captains were knowledgeable about the Auckland Islands and the specific perils of sailing in and around them.

In spite of this, I will stipulate that both the *Grafton* and *Invercauld* crews found themselves in a disaster that was, for the sake of my purposes, unavoidable. Lacking evidence to support it, I will not assume that Captain Musgrave's shipwreck was beyond his control, or that Captain Dalgarno could or should have done something differently to avoid his shipwreck. I will say that both captains, using the technology they had at the time, found themselves in situations where they had no reasonable way of knowing they would run aground. We will give them an even start from the point of grounding.

The Captain's Role

So, you've just metaphorically shipwrecked, in life or in business. What decisions must be made immediately to ensure survival? How will you get food? How will you make a shelter? How will you organize yourselves to coordinate efforts? A critical first decision is who will be in charge. One of the rules of the sea states the captain of the ship is the ultimate authority, literally a dictator. Sterling Hayden said it this way, "A sailing ship is no democracy; you don't caucus a crew as to where you'll go any more than you inquire when they'd like to shorten sail."

The captain doesn't get everyone around and say, "Okay, guys, I was thinking we might go to this destination. What does everybody think? Let's take a vote."

No. The captain says, "We're going in this direction."

He then orders the ship to go in that direction, and everybody goes along with him because he's the captain. However, this only remains true in the context of an intact ship and crew. Even a landing party going ashore is still under the captain's authority. As soon as the ship wrecks, however, the captain and crew are no longer shipmates; they are now all castaways. This is a very important distinction as we look at the details of these two wrecks in particular. When you are shipwrecked, the rules of sea go out the window, and you are now an individual or a band of survivors, hopefully working together to survive.

Democracy vs. Dictatorship

Captain Musgrave made a significant decision of leadership. Although he initially did give orders, he recognized that all five *Grafton* survivors were in this situation equally. With Raynal's urging, Musgrave recognized he no longer had the right to be the ultimate authority over his men. Even if he was a good man, even if he was a fair man, even if he really took the interests of those other four men to heart, he accepted that, as a fellow castaway, he didn't have the right to rule dictatorially.

After Raynal offered the suggestion of electing a leader and sensing the democratic way would be best for the group, Musgrave decided to yield, effectively saying, "Okay, men, you're no longer my crew. We're all castaways in this mess, equally. So, we have to work together and come up with how we're going to survive this. We need to decide amongst ourselves who will be our leader in the tough times ahead. In most situations, we can let the majority rule, but, if we have a situation where somebody has to make a decision, we need a leader."

Because he had been a good captain and exhibited good leadership, good decision-making during the voyage, was willing to join them as equals, and had been sharing in the workload from the moment of the shipwreck, the other four unanimously elected him their leader.

Now, contrast that with Captain Dalgarno of the *Invercauld*. From the very beginning, everything he did and said was selfish to the extreme. Even though he maintained a dictatorial role as captain after the wreck, he could at least have been making benevolent decisions to ensure the survival of the other eighteen men. Instead, he ordered his men around for only his survival and his comfort.

Good Leaders Work for the Good of the Crew

This first point of leadership is revealed in this stark contrast between Captain Musgrave and Captain Dalgarno. In a crisis, how do you respond? Please note I would never advocate for the CEO of a company to relinquish control in a crisis. As CEO of Goldleaf, I would never have said, "Okay, we're in a crisis, so I'm not the CEO anymore. Let's take a vote and decide who's going to be the CEO of this company." That's not the parallel I'm drawing. However, in a time of crisis, the CEO has to do some important things that exhibit leadership with benevolence and care for the stakeholders (i.e., employees, customers, and stockholders).

First, as CEO, you have to make sure your people know, not just assume they know, that you are looking out for all of their benefits. They need to know you're doing things for the benefit of the whole team to survive the crisis, not just yourself or the owners. You have to specifically say and do things that make it overtly evident to every single employee that you are looking out after each and every one of them, that the decisions you're making take into account their well-being, jobs, and roles. One of the ways to do that is by seeking out more advice, more input from employees, in a professional, reasonable way.

If you're in a crisis situation, you may not immediately know what to do, so you look for those additional sources of information. Reach out, bring people together and ask for advice if your emergency allows for that. "Hey, we're in a tight spot here. What do you guys think?" This shows employees you genuinely care about them and value their expertise.

I recall at one point, early in Goldleaf's history, we had a robust product, but a brand-new operating system (OS) had just been released. There was much discussion about whether the new OS was a stable enough platform for us to rely on as a customer-facing application. As more pressure came to create a version supporting that OS, I solicited the opinion of the development team. One developer stated that he could create a prototype while still maintaining his coding responsibilities. I agreed, and over the next couple of months I regularly checked in to learn of the progress of this effort. We eventually did create and distribute the prototype product, and by the time we created a full cloud-based version several years later, over ten thousand copies of the "prototype" product had been delivered.

Another way to show you have their best interests at heart is to stay with employees who work late to figure out a problem or finish a project. Visit them individually, asking, "Hey, how are you guys doing?" I can't tell you how many times I ordered food or brought in whatever resources I thought might assist my crew working late hours. Those actions send a message: "Hey, this boss genuinely cares about us individually, not just about how we can get this problem solved for his company."

If they don't know you have their best interests at heart, they might be more tempted to act in self-preservation. Employees may make decisions not in the best interest of the group or the company. By making sure they know you have their best interests at heart, you can help your team focus on fixing the problem and coming up with solutions that are for the greater good.

You've already demonstrated as a leader that you're committed to their preservation, right? In the case of a shipwreck, that means you, as the leader, are seeking immediate shelter, food, safety, etc. In the case of a company crisis, that means rallying the troops to seek out root causes and leading the effort to create solutions while consistently encouraging all team members and assuring them of the company's ability to survive this crisis.

At the end of the day, employees who are willing to do whatever it takes to resolve the crisis will make the difference. Your leadership is not so much about figuring out the solution, but ensuring your people are in the right frame of mind to do so.

Everyone's My Boss

One thing I have learned throughout my career is that, regardless of where I was in the organizational chart of the many organizations I worked for, I would always have a boss. One person was always my direct supervisor, somebody I had to answer to, report to, interact with, and take direction from. When I became CEO of Goldleaf Technologies, I came to realize this was still true, but the roles were reversed.

People might say, "Oh, you didn't have a boss. You *were* the boss."

No. *Everybody* became my boss.

The idea that a CEO need only focus on those five to eight chief lieutenants reporting to him or her is ridiculous. As the CEO, everybody becomes your boss. When I was in a position to oversee one particular department of an organization, I would exclusively focus on the people who were directly reporting to me and others in my department. While I was still interested in what went on in other parts of the organization, I was primarily focused on the areas I was responsible for, my direct supervision.

When I became the CEO, I couldn't say, "Oh, I'm going to pay attention to the marketing group more than I pay attention to the customer support group or the operations group." This feeling of responsibility is difficult to describe to people who have never been in charge of an entire company, particularly one that grew to have dozens, hundreds, or in some cases, many thousands of employees. All of a sudden, you feel a direct responsibility for everybody. If somebody's spouse is hurt in an accident or some other tragedy happens, you are aware of that. You pay attention to that. The good CEOs, and I certainly ascribe to this as well, make sure they connect with their employees, that people see them, hear from them, not just in periodic meetings in the normal course of business, but also in a day-to-day way, getting around the office spaces, not ensconced in whatever corporate suite of offices they have.

Of course, this gets harder to do as the company grows. If you have thousands of employees, you have to work harder to make sure you are still in touch with each employee in some meaningful way. Maybe instead of one-on-ones, you do some group breakfast or lunch meetings. Maybe you periodically drop in on division meetings. Maybe you write a personal note to an employee whose spouse was in an accident. Staying in touch at a personal level is critically important.

Admit Your Mistakes

Sometimes, you have to admit a mistake to show your team how important they are in the midst of the crisis. If Captain Musgrave of the *Grafton* made a strategic error that led to their grounding, he might have said, "Men, I apologize. My error led to this disaster." Sometimes, it may be as simple as admitting you were at fault and saying, "Okay, this is the situation we're in. Here's how we're going to band together, and here are the things we need to do. Let's gather some input, some data, and figure out what our options are from here."

Leaders who refuse to admit when they make an error are deluding themselves that their crew doesn't realize who is at fault. Trust me, they know. By admitting when we are at fault, we are not lessening our role as a leader or as a decision-maker. We are acknowledging our human frailty. And, in my experience, employees respond well when a leader says, "It's my fault. I apologize. Now, let's work together to affect a positive resolution." Employees will go to battle more readily for that type of leader.

Active Participation

Musgrave directed his men to immediately secure sources of food and create a reasonable structure to live in. He also actively participated in all survival activities; he wasn't just bossing the men around. As soon as safely possible, they went back out to the ship, retrieving as much useful material as they could. They were able to secure Raynal's gun, some ammunition, and tobacco. Ultimately, they harvested the physical structure of the boat itself: sails, rope, line, wood planks, and so forth.

So, one other advantage that Captain Musgrave had over Captain Dalgarno was that his grounded ship was more readily available.

The Grafton survivors were able to scavenge the ship
—Alfred De Neuville Engraving, Public Domain—

Dalgarno and his men were huddled around in a big, pitiful mass without any real plan for how they were going to set up and survive.

So, in a crisis, consider this idea of evaluating resources. What information can we gather? What are possible courses of action? How do we involve all of the relevant staff in the recovery process? What decisions or courses of action will sustain us until we can get ourselves in a position for a permanent solution?

Activity toward a common goal is a great motivator. For your business, this activity may be the creation and updating of a Disaster Recovery Plan. Not only is it important to cover every possible contingency in this document, but also to regularly keep it updated. For the *Grafton*, the common goal translated into decision-making about how they set up signals for passing ships and other activities related to being rescued. Captain Musgrave did a lot of those things earlier in the process than Captain Dalgarno, who made selfish decisions.

A critical task – setting a signal flag
—Alfred De Neuville Engraving, Public Domain—

Making Hard Decisions

When it came time to leave in the refurbished dinghy for New Zealand, Musgrave knew he had to make an executive decision about who would go and who would stay. If you were Musgrave in this situation, would you pick the two you would take with you, which by default would also select the two to leave behind? Or would you have done something else, like draw straws?

Think about this from Musgrave's perspective. He's got four men: Raynal, who exhibited great skill and was their savior in terms of all the things he did on the island; Alick, a master seaman; George, a seaman; and Henry the cook. Musgrave needed men to sail the vessel. If he drew straws, he might wind up with Henry the cook and George the less-qualified seaman.

Musgrave chooses Harris and Forge to stay behind on the island
—Alfred De Neuville Engraving, Public Domain—

A Big Difference

The contrast in leadership between Musgrave and Dalgarno is stark. Let's examine more of the differences between these two captains in their decision-making and leadership.

Issue	Captain Musgrave	Captain Dalgarno
Immediate Orders	Organized the crew to get to shore safely. Secured sources of food and shelter.	Was seemingly incapacitated and gave no orders. Conducted no action in support of his men.
Attitude Toward Crew	Organized and delegated work specific to survival. Delegated authority.	Ordered the two surviving ship's boys to attend to his personal needs... until they died.
Encouragement of Esprit de Corps	Supported idea to elect a leader. Organized nightly education sessions, Bible study.	None. In fact, his selfish actions angered the men.
Organization and Safety	Ensured safe arrival from shipwreck for all men. Carefully planned hunting expeditions.	Allowed men to go off alone or in groups with no direction or organization. Many of these men never returned or were found dead.
Effort toward Possible Rescue	Was actively involved in watching for/ signaling passing ships.	Took no action. Allowed/ ordered Robert Holding to conduct all survival activities.
Ultimate Rescue	Sailed a modified dinghy to New Zealand with two of the crew. Came back to get the other two men left behind.	Was rescued with Holding and Smith through no effort of his own. Sixteen other survivors of the wreck died.

A Bad Example

There are many examples of people in authority showing the opposite of good leadership. Remember the disaster of the cruise ship *Costa Concordia* back in 2012? The captain took the ship far out of the channel off the coast of Isola del Giglio in Italy to show off and accidentally ripped a hole in the hull. The ship took on water and began listing. Many people died in that incident, but the captain compounded the bad decision by abandoning ship while there were still passengers on board. This is the capstone of poor leadership from a captain (or CEO): save yourself while ignoring your passengers (customers) and your crew (employees).

Another example is the Lotus 123 debacle. In the 1990s, an error occurred in the software which made a value incorrect if the decimal stretched more than eight digits. Rather than own up to the bug and immediately engineer a fix, the company decided to continue shipping the defective software and countered criticism with the logic of, "How many people need to calculate out to that many significant digits anyway?" The scorn and ridicule they received lasted much longer than the fix for the program. I am sure the executive(s) involved in making the initial decision to shirk their responsibility felt they were saving the company money, but it rarely works out that way. Ducking the responsibility to do the right thing in the first place nearly always costs more, in money or reputation.

Individual Leadership

So far in this chapter, I've focused on the captains and how leaders should react in a crisis, but I also want to draw attention to individual leadership and the related decision-making process. As an individual, you may not be responsible for any other person. You may not be a supervisor or manager over anyone else. Does that mean you don't have an opportunity to exhibit leadership? Not at all! Every day, there are countless opportunities for self-leadership. People who exhibit good personal leadership and who, subsequently, make good decisions related to that are then viewed as more valuable in general by the companies that employ them.

Opportunities for Personal Networking

Do you have a group of people you go to lunch with all the time or socialize with? Are there other people you don't connect with in the company? You rarely speak to those other employees on a one-on-one basis, learning more about them, befriending them, or including them in discussions. Maybe you're working on something and consistently have questions that you take to one of your friends. "Hey, I'm wrestling with this. Can you help me understand this particular concept?" There may be four other people in that department, but you're not really friendly with them, so you don't ever reach out to them. However, you can start exhibiting individual leadership if you make the effort to connect to others you don't normally speak to.

Start by interacting with others within your organization. Create some reasons to meet with them. Maybe at some time in the future when you are called upon to exhibit some leadership or make some decisions, you will have a better frame of reference concerning these other people. You will know these people and their skills better. Maybe you reach out to somebody in accounting who isn't ordinarily somebody you interact with, but you made a point to ask him some questions or interact with him. You learn some things about another employee's skills and experiences.

Later, you're in a situation where a senior leader is saying, "Hey, look, we need somebody who has these kinds of skills." You're included in that group, and you raise your hand. "Well, I know

Smith from over in accounting has the kind of skills you're talking about." Now everybody's looking at you like you have a second head, right? "How do you know about Smith?" You know because you've spent time with Smith, conversing and asking questions.

Being Prepared to Have Input

Even though you're not a manager of any kind, you are in a position where an open question is asked within the group, and you have some information to share. All of a sudden, the senior leader who may not even know that much about you, depending on the size of your organization, now thinks, "Wow. That was pretty impressive." If you're not a senior leader or manager, you may have no idea how people in leadership positions look at their employees and make decisions on a going-forward basis about who are the stars, who are the rising stars, who are the potential stars, and who are people who are just taking up seats.

Companies go through down periods. They go through times when they have to make hard decisions, and because of the economy and downturn in business, they may say, "We have to cut ten percent of our workforce." Do you want a better-than-even chance of not being in the group who's cut? Say there are five people in your department. All five are great performers who do the same amount of work, but one of them has to go. It will come down to these intangibles. The leadership will ask, "Who exhibits potential for leadership? Who has shown they can make good decisions?"

When they get around to discussing the final decision, it will be similar to the managers of a sports team. "Okay, we're going to keep this person over that person based on these other intangibles they've shown." For example, a baseball manager would want an infielder who could also play right field, or even pitch if needed. Even as an individual, you have great incentive to consistently use and exercise good judgment, sound decision-making principles, and personal leadership that helps you into this group of rising stars, and maybe move up in the company or parlay those experiences into a better management position at another company. Each individual decision can be as important as a CEO making a global decision.

Future Impact

Another important thing to consider is the long-lasting impacts of poor leadership and poor decision-making. This equally applies whether you're a manager or an individual exhibiting personal leadership. Even though Captain Dalgarno made all those horrible decisions, he left the island earlier than Captain Musgrave's crew, sailing away on the *Julian*, which deposited the three *Invercauld* survivors in Peru, South America. There, he reported to British authorities and told his version of the shipwreck of the *Invercauld*. It is interesting that he specifically told Robert Holding to tell no one anything about their time on Auckland Island.

A reporter interviewed Dalgarno and published the story that was picked up by papers throughout the world. When Musgrave returned to civilization, he was shocked to find out there had been other castaways on the island at the same time. Musgrave had a much better tale to tell, but a lot of people were already mesmerized by Dalgarno's account. Now, consider what happened with those two individuals afterward. Because first mate Andrew Smith survived (and perhaps since Dalgarno left for England, leaving Smith in Peru), Smith was able to tell the same reporter a more accurate story about the fate of the *Invercauld*, including how Dalgarno actually behaved, and that account was also widely published.

Musgrave went on to have a distinguished career, was given charge of another ship, and had success both with the book he wrote of the Auckland Island ordeal, and as a working captain, before retiring and returning to England. Captain Dalgarno returned to England but did not get another commission.

If you exhibit poor leadership traits, whether as a manager or as an individual (unless the company is poorly run, which is an obvious possibility these days), you won't likely get offered future leadership positions. Even in today's environment, where people are guarded about what they will or will not say to somebody calling for a reference concerning a potential hire, usually there's a way to express that this person exhibited poor leadership skills or poor decision-making. Those are two crucial skills, particularly for anyone desiring to be a manager. If you want to be considered for more challenging positions in your career to grow and expand your opportunities, be especially careful about how you exercise leadership and make decisions, because those will be noticed by supervisors, management, and business owners.

Think Harder, Speak Softer

Consider this principle: "In a time of crisis, think harder and speak softer." I am not a fan of a leader who yells, screams, and throws things to motivate people. All things being equal, that style is not generally effective. There are clearly exceptions, like Steve Jobs, who literally acted like a crazy person but was so brilliant that people stuck with him. But, I think for the most part, unless you are exceptionally brilliant, you can't get away with bizarre or irrational behavior.

However, what if you are generally loud and boisterous? You're garrulous. You have a big personality. I would certainly consider myself more loud than quiet. Almost everyone who's ever been around me or works with me says my voice carries. In the past, people have come and closed my office door and wondered, "Why can't that guy be quieter?"

So, in a time of crisis, I don't think going louder is the answer. I must speak softly, especially in a time of crisis. Generally, when you speak quietly, people listen more intently. They are hyper-focused on what you're saying. You will have greater impact, not only because they have to carefully listen, but also because you're normally speaking much louder. They can't help but take note of the difference in volume. I think it gives an attitude of confidence and control. Even in a situation where you may not feel competent or in control, you will give employees the idea that you are.

Having said all that, you cannot be someone you are not. If you are not the type of person who would be quieter, it does not follow that you are not a good leader. Be true to yourself. Identify your bad traits and minimize them as much as possible, particularly in a crisis. And, in your way, make sure everyone knows you care deeply about customers, employees, and shareholders.

Think harder. What does that mean? Consider what Albert Einstein's said about having an hour to solve a problem. He would spend fifty-five minutes thinking about the problem and five minutes creating a solution. We've already mentioned certain situations that require immediate action; you don't have the equivalent of fifty-five out of sixty minutes to think. But, given those exceptions, you should be thinking extremely hard about the actual problem in a crisis.

Where's the best place to think? Whether you're a manager or just an individual, you need to put yourself in the best possible place of thinking. Trying to think in a meeting room with fifteen other people all talking at the same time may not be the best environment. Consider giving your people the freedom, the luxury, of being able to step away and think. Let's say you have a crisis and have assembled your team in the conference room. You explain the problem and say, "Give me your ideas for resolution." That puts everyone on the spot to create a solution. Without the requisite time for them to research and think, it's likely their initial responses will not be the most thoughtful, reasoned options.

A better procedure would be to assemble the team, lay out the problem, and provide them a specific amount of time to research and think. Then reassemble the team and discuss the problem and potential solutions. It is the rare employee who, when challenged to give an on-the-spot response, would say, "I do not have enough information to comment. Let me research and think about this. I'll get back with you by the end of the day."

By the way, if you have an employee who says that, you should probably track them for future advancement.

And if you agree that thinking is an important activity, consider building "thinking time" into the regular activities of your employees. Proactive thinking might yield specific activities and processes that avoid future disasters. Just remember not to blast anyone who is actually thinking, but *appears* to be doing something else, like sleeping, daydreaming, or goofing off.

Left Brain/Right Brain Thinking

Numerous studies describe the function of the right half and left half of your brain. Our left brain handles things in an automated mode. The right brain is much more contemplative and doesn't yield immediate conclusions given the input. Also, the right brain is dominated by the left brain. The right brain can solve complex problems but only if the left brain gets "distracted" and gives it a chance to think.

As a strategic planning facilitator, I have conducted numerous strategic thinking exercises such as getting people to draw using their right brain, using the techniques outlined in the book *Drawing on the Right Side of the Brain* by Betty Edwards.

Have you experienced this right brain/left brain dichotomy? Maybe a song was playing on the radio and somebody asked you, "Hey, who sings that song?" You knew that you knew the artist, but you couldn't bring to mind the name, so you thought about it hard for a few minutes and then the conversation went on and you forgot about it.

Did you really forget about it? No. In fact, your right brain was still working the problem. The next morning when you were in the shower, all of a sudden the name of the singer comes to you. Your left brain was concentrating on doing your morning grooming schedule and boom! Here comes the singer's name. That might have been fourteen hours later. Your right brain was figuring out how to collect that information wherever it was stored to bring it back to your conscious thought.

The way we engaged the right brain at Goldleaf was with Ping-Pong. We had a room at Goldleaf with a Ping-Pong table and a bunch of white boards all around. If you were stuck on a problem and played Ping-Pong for a time, the left brain had to focus on hitting the ball and was consumed with playing the game. Thus, the right brain was freed to work on that problem. I can't tell you how many times somebody had the "eureka" moment, ran over to the whiteboard, and wrote something down or got people together to discuss a solution.

So, you must give yourself the opportunity to effectively think, not just mentally wander. Some of that thinking could happen with groupthink in a mutual brainstorming session. I do a lot of strategic planning, so I realize how valuable those sessions can be.

But sometimes, before a brainstorming session, you need to give people individual time to think, and then they can come to the brainstorming session with ideas or potential solutions that came out of their own individual thinking as opposed to this big, on-the-spot groupthink.

Leadership Not Made by Crisis

Author Robert Freeman wrote that "Character is not made by crisis; it is only exhibited." I think we can substitute the word "character" with the word "leadership."

Certainly character is a big part of leadership, but I don't want to divert down that path. Let's focus on the idea that leadership is not built in a crisis—it's revealed. People who have taken opportunities to show leadership in the past, either as a manager overseeing other people or just as an individual, have practiced making decisions and taking action.

Collectively, the decisions and actions leading up to that point of crisis build the person's leadership qualities. I don't believe someone lacking leadership skills will suddenly develop them in a time of crisis. Are there possible examples of somebody who had never exhibited any kind of leadership and then exhibited some? Sure. There is the example of Robert Holding, a common seaman on the *Invercauld*, who kept himself and the two senior officers alive on Auckland Island.

However, most people start small, learning, showing leadership in a number of areas, making good decisions and growing into more leadership, even though they are not necessarily managing people or working in any official position of leadership. Those people will generally exhibit effective leadership in a crisis because they prepared themselves to do so.

For the crew of the *Grafton*, their very lives depended on the leadership and decision-making of Captain Musgrave, while sixteen sailors from the *Invercauld* died, almost certainly due to the weak leadership and non-existent decision-making of Captain Dalgarno.

Do you work for a Musgrave or a Dalgarno? Would you consider making a job change based on the type of leader who is in charge of your current organization? Are you personally a Musgrave or a Dalgarno? What would it take to get you to evolve from a Dalgarno to a Musgrave?

CHAPTER FIVE

Taking Corrective Action

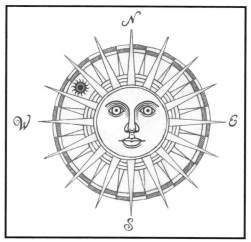

"Never assume the obvious is true."

— William Safire

My dad set a new course northeast and told us we should see land in about three hours. The wind direction and strength was favorable for us to progress under sail. We had nice weather and were hopeful that we were very close to having the vacation we had planned: fun in the sun, diving off the boat and snorkeling for conch. After four hours had passed with no sight of land, we became uneasy again. My dad felt like we must be close and kept on going.

On our trip aboard the *Alacrity*, it would have been irrational for us to make a course change after four hours of sailing if we had determined it would take five hours to reach our destination. What about the flipside of this same issue? Based on the sextant reading, we had a firm belief of where we were, and it placed us on the chart in a specific location. We said, "We've got to turn northeast, and if we go northeast and sail at the rate of speed that we're able to sail, it will take about three hours in order to get to West End."

Off we went! We headed on that course. All the information we had, not just from the compass and the sextant, but even the position of the sun since it was now daylight, told us we were going northeast. Even if we assumed the Bermuda Triangle had somehow played with the magnetic field and our compass was not working correctly, the sun rises in the east and moves west across the sky, so we could find ninety degrees from the sun, split that in half, and head in that direction.

We could say with some confidence, "We're sailing northeast." Assuming our starting position was correct, we were on the path to problem resolution. In three hours, we expected to see West End.

Three hours went by. We didn't see West End.

However, we didn't say, "Well, it's right at three hours. No Bahamas. Stop! Stop right here. We're going to make an immediate correction." No, because the calculations for sailing are not that precise. We estimated it would be three hours, so we continued to go forward.

Three hours and fifteen minutes went by. No Bahamas.

Three hours and thirty minutes. No Bahamas.

In hindsight, we should have been taking sextant readings every hour. Perhaps every half hour. After all, we had a reason to be suspicious of our position as that was the original problem we encountered that morning. And yet, inexplicably, we relied on that one reading to reset our course.

Four hours passed.

Wait a minute. We were confident of our speed. We were even more confident of our direction. If, in fact, our starting location was accurate, we absolutely should have seen land, or we would have run aground by now based on where we thought we were. With renewed confidence of our direction, the only logical conclusion was that our starting position that morning was wrong.

Making Calculations

After enough time passes to satisfy yourself that the course of action is not working toward a positive conclusion, then you have to stop at that point, take stock, and take corrective action. You wouldn't say, "Okay, we said if we were going six knots per hour we would reach West End, but, hey, maybe we're not really going six knots." You can't make up facts to support the theory you're going in the right direction. We knew what our speed was because we had a speed gauge indicating our speed through the water. Separate from the gauge, we used a technique where you can determine how fast you're going by dropping a piece of paper off the bow of the boat and timing how long it takes to get to the stern.[4]

Well, how can you know what is fact? In my example, what was not fact was our starting location. However, we got that information from using the sextant. We're assuming that, a) Dad used the sextant correctly, and b) there were no other factors relating to our use of the sextant that would have put us in a different

---

4 Speed = Distance divided by Time, since the end goal is calculating speed. Say your boat is forty feet long, and you know the time it takes a piece of paper to float from the bow to the stern is five seconds, then you can calculate the speed by dividing distance by time (40 feet/5 seconds – 8 feet per second). There are 3,600 seconds in an hour. So 8 X 3,600 yields 29,280 feet per hour. Divide that by 5,280 (the number of feet per mile) and you get 5.55 miles per hour. Note: this calculation is for speed over water (SOW) and doesn't account for other factors (side currents, tacking back and forth, etc.) that would affect speed over ground (SOG).

location.[5] When you're in a boat in the middle of the ocean, you are fairly devoid of specific information. You take a 360-degree look, and there's just a bunch of water. There's no reference to any meaningful information.

Too Reliant on Technology

This raises the issue of how reliant we have become on techno-gadgetry, even in software development. We have tools at our disposal that assist in debugging or checking for potential problems and badly written code, but sometimes those systems themselves aren't working properly, are configured incorrectly, or just fail. So, you have to be careful how much you rely on technology. Expecting a different result after continuing to do the same thing over and over again with no other variables changing is the definition of insanity (thanks to Mr. Einstein for that bit of wisdom!).

In the case of the *Alacrity*, we continued to sail on well past the time frame we should have seen land. We continued northeast, thinking perhaps our course was correct, but maybe we were a little further southwest of where we wanted to be. Therefore, it would have taken us longer. We convinced ourselves we needed to let the plan go forward, when in fact every minute, every mile we continued on that course could be taking us further and further away from the actual goal. The key here is: when you have good evidence that the information you've used in order to make a decision is no longer valid, you must stop and re-evaluate. You must say, "If the data I used to make a decision was accurate, I will see some evidence of a positive result occurring within this period of time." If you don't get that evidence, then you have to do something different.

---

5 Three basic errors can occur when using a sextant. Sailors use the letters PSI to remind them of these errors. P—the Perpendicular Error where the index mirror is not perpendicular to the plane of the instrument. S—the Side Error where the horizon mirror is not perpendicular to the instrument. I—the Index Error, where the horizon mirror and the index mirror are not parallel with each other.

False Hope

In the Goldleaf crisis, we had a particular problem that caused the ACH Client system to run slowly for no apparent reason. I used all the resources available to come up with multiple possibilities that could cause the system to slow. Then I started making changes in the system to see whether or not they had any desired effect in reducing the lag. We actually did a number of those things, and, quite frankly, some of them appeared as if they were having some effect, which raises an issue—sometimes your efforts can compound a problem. There's the solution to the problem, which completely makes it go away, and then there are other solutions you try that don't really fix the problem but may ameliorate the symptoms, making it appear that something positive is happening, when in fact the underlying problem itself hasn't gone away.

We experienced this at Goldleaf. We'd implement a code change that showed some promise, and we began to think the solution was down that path. We could have or should have gathered more empirical evidence concerning what we were seeing related to the slowness, so we could know whether or not we were addressing the real problem or seeing some improvements in the processing speed without actually fixing the problem. Taking actions to "improve" the process when the only sources of variation present are common causes of variation will actually increase the variability in the process and lead to a deterioration in performance. You can isolate common causes of variation in a process through experimentation and testing, and then take systemic actions to reduce or eliminate those common-cause sources of variation.

Without experimental analysis, you will almost always do more harm than good. The sources of variation are so intermingled that your interpretation of what is happening can be completely wrong. Unfortunately, we didn't set down specific milestones to indicate we were making progress toward resolution.

We should have said, "If we're truly addressing the problem, we expect to see evidence of a positive result." For example, we might have said, "A known test cycle will run at a specific rate of speed. A ping to a known endpoint would return in a specific timeframe. A database subroutine would return a specific set of results in a specific timeframe." If all three of those milestones are not observed, then we're not addressing the problem, we're simply seeing some symptomatic results. Because we didn't do that, we wound up delaying the discovery of the real solution past the time frame that would have made a difference.

A Constant Process

At the point you decide the current status is no longer working, you have to take stock and say, "What do I absolutely know? And am I basing that knowledge on assumption? What are those assumptions?" Assumptions can be incorrect. Facts cannot be incorrect, but you can misinterpret them. Going back to the *Alacrity* story, the speed at which we were moving through the water was fact. The direction we were going was a fact, not because we had the compass, but because we had a visual sighting of where we were headed in relation to the morning sun. We could rely on those as facts and be confident we were not misinterpreting them. We assumed our starting position, the proverbial "X" on the map, was also fact, based on the sextant readings.

When we got to that two-and-a-half-hour mark where we should have seen land, we could have stopped and taken another sextant reading. If it indicated we were still on the correct path but farther away, we could continue. If we had done this several times, at some point we would have had to realize the laws of physics say we can't keep being that far away if we're traveling at a known rate of speed. Constantly ascertain where you are, then separate facts—the concrete things you know, either independently verified or with multiple pieces of verification that give you an idea that something is true—from assumptions—information that could be wrong and facts you have misinterpreted.

This is a constant process: working through the problem, making sure you don't unnecessarily delay action, knowing when to stop and gather new information or confirm facts, gathering all the facts you can ascertain and confirm to be facts, and examining all assumptions to determine which of them are, or could be, untrue. Then, gather the necessary information to confirm assumptions as facts or fictions. If you have established facts from assumptions, take the information you have and make the reasonable next best course correction or decision to do something different. Don't continue in a direction that will prove unfruitful.

Decision Formula

Applying this principle, here is a simple formula that you can apply to any personal or business situation:

1) Based on {Fact A} and {Fact B} and {Assumption C} = You will take X course of action.

2) If a proposed course of action is working, it will yield the following evidence: Milestone A in X time frame, Milestone B in Y time frame, Milestone C in Z time frame.

3) While X, Y, and Z time frames are in process, work toward ascertaining if any facts are being misinterpreted or assumptions are being accepted without challenge. If you have reasonable evidence that any of the information you are relying on is inaccurate, immediately stop and return to number one. Reformulate a revised course of action.

4) If the evidence milestones you have set do not show you are working toward a positive result, immediately stop and return to number one. Reformulate a revised course of action.

Returning to Home Base

Another interesting point I want to make here relevant to problem-solving is the idea of whether or not continuing to the goal is warranted. Think about this. We were trying to get to West End, Bahamas. That was our goal. Yet, when the sun came up that morning and there was no sign of the island, we had other options available to us. Regardless of any issues with the compass, we could have turned around and headed due west.

What would that have done? We knew for a fact that, based on the amount of time we had sailed, if we turned and sailed due west, we were going to reach the coast of Florida. It's a really big, long state! It's over five hundred miles from Jacksonville down to Key West. I don't care how far south we had gone in our track on the *Alacrity*; we hadn't gone far enough that we were going to miss Florida if we sailed west.

Since we didn't know where we were, it would have been entirely reasonable and rational to say, "You know what? We're lost. We don't really know where we are. We think based on taking this sextant reading that we're here, but we're not really sure that's true. If we head west, we will reach the coast of Florida. Once we are in sight of Florida, we will know exactly where we are because we know all the landmarks."

From there, we could have just sailed along the coast back to West Palm Beach and said, "Wow, that was a weird, kinda freaky thing that happened. We followed our normal procedures but didn't make it to West End." We could have laughed about it later and said, "Wow. What happened? It's the Bermuda Triangle! Our compass got all screwed up."

That option was entirely possible but never discussed, never thought about, never considered. Maybe my dad thought of it. If he did, he never said anything, and to this day he does not remember if he considered this option. It never occurred to us to abandon our goal of getting to West End, Bahamas, and actually return to the United States.

If I'm planning how I'm going to address a disaster, one of the things I have to be prepared to do is to go back to home base, to return to Stage 1. In the case of software development, typically things go wrong when you're changing something. Software is not static; it doesn't remain the same. You're constantly adding enhancements. You add a new patch, a new feature. You're fixing some other bug, you're putting in some other kind of enhancement. In the process of doing that, even with all your best efforts to test and provide quality assurance that you're not breaking something else, when you put it into production, you will have broken something. The system's not operating the way it used to. Any software company worth its salt will have a procedure to roll back to the code set they knew was working, figure out what they broke, and fix that. That's the equivalent of turning the sailboat around and heading to Florida, so you have a starting place you know is sound. Then figure out what you need to do to avoid that error again.

We didn't think of that when we were on the *Alacrity;* we just kept on going. You could say, "Hey, your compass was wonky, so how would you know you're going west anyway?" We had a separate piece of information: the sun's position.

Knowing exactly where you are, that position on the map, and stopping to take stock is all about ascertaining information you know to be true, not just information you assume to be true. Sometimes, it might be necessary for you to take a couple of steps backwards in order to get to a place you know. Then you can make necessary corrections from there.

CHAPTER SIX
The Crew

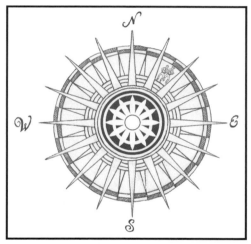

*"Whatever you do in life, surround yourself with smart
people who'll argue with you."*

— John Wooden

In the story of the *Invercauld* and the *Grafton*, we can learn from
how the crew was chosen. Unfortunately, the historical record
doesn't show any detail about how Captain Dalgarno of the *Invercauld* chose his crew. We can assume he used the typical process
and looked for people with the types of skills required to sail the

particular vessel they were taking. The *Invercauld* was a much bigger ship, sailing with thirty plus sailors, whereas the *Grafton* was smaller with a crew of only five. I imagine Dalgarno chose a couple of key lieutenants and a first mate but, other than those hires, it's likely that he didn't personally hire the rest of the crew. Choosing a sailing crew in the 1860s centered first and foremost on the basic needs of sailing a vessel.

Raynal, A Great Example

Captain Musgrave of the *Grafton* used a similar process in terms of hiring his crew. However, when you read more about the crew's survival, you find first mate François Raynal was a critical addition to the *Grafton* expedition.

Raynal was somebody Musgrave knew had a skill set that went beyond basic sailing knowledge and the particular focus of the expedition. As you read in Chapter 2, they originally set out to look for this special type of ore that contained argentiferous tin.

Engraving of Raynal by Alphonse de Neuville

Francois Raynal - Wicked smart and resourceful

Raynal, from his days prospecting in the Australian goldfields, had specific knowledge about the tin and the ore in which it would be contained, as well as how to search for it. He also had some knowledge of Campbell Island, which was purported to have this tin. These are certainly some of the reasons why he was a part of the crew. But, Musgrave also knew that Raynal was well-educated and a skilled engineer. Even though Musgrave had no idea how those skills might be applied or how useful they may be, there's no question he considered Raynal extremely valuable as a first mate based on all of those additional skills. There are many advantages to having a big crew relative to the kinds of specialization you can get. But, if your crew is small, you must get people who are well-rounded.

Knowing How You Hire

If you're a CEO, then your crew extends beyond your direct reports and involves everybody in the company. While you may not be directly involved in interviewing and hiring all the way down to those different levels, you certainly must be aware of the hiring process. The effective leader will take a personal interest in the hiring of people who will have any leadership position in your company.

In a book called *The Virgin Way*, author Richard Branson highlights the importance of being involved in the interview of key managers, regardless of whether they report directly to you or not. With over fifty thousand employees across numerous product lines, you can imagine how difficult this must be for Mr. Branson (although, as he says in the book, he often invites these potential employees to come see him at his private island in the British Virgin Islands, and none of them have ever refused to do so). More importantly, working in close association with your head of HR and your direct reports, you must ensure you are imparting your values, goals, and desires relative to how the organization acquires talent.

If you're a senior manager, something like executive vice-president, or senior vice-president, you likely have multiple managers under you. Hopefully, you're getting direction—the goals and values for hiring new employees—from your CEO. You're imbibing these values and passing them to all your supervisors downstream. Picking the right crew is a critical step, so take the time to get this right.

But what if you're not a manager? You're out there just doing your job. And that job is important to the overall success of the enterprise. Maybe you have a specialized skill. You're a scientist or a computer programmer, but you have no supervisory role whatsoever. You don't have even one person who reports to you. Does this mean the concepts I'm describing don't apply to you all? I would say they do.

In many business environments, you will be working with other employees, or perhaps with outside vendors or consultants. Those could constitute a crew.

You might work as a cross-functional group within the company where you are closely collaborating with other employees and contractors. You might be in a position to exert influence over them. You may even have the opportunity to choose who is on that crew on a project-by-project basis. You may be asked to put together a cross-functional team for a particular project, to go outside of your particular area of the company and find others in the company with a different perspective to be a part of this team.

So, you put together this team, and maybe you and your crew tackle a vexing problem or do some brainstorming. In the context of your everyday work life or certainly over a period of weeks, months, or years, you could have the opportunity to pick a crew. Think about who you're bringing together to work alongside you in these different activities as if you were a senior manager or

CEO. Don't ignore these concepts of carefully choosing a crew just because today you're not a manager.

Your Personal Crew

What if you examine leadership from a personal standpoint? Let's step aside from the business world for a minute and talk about us as individuals and who our "crew" is. Obviously, we have people we choose to be a part of our crew. Probably the closest relationship would be your spouse. You don't pick your parents. You don't generally get to pick your children, though you are responsible for them. But your spouse is somebody you choose to be a part of your crew. Then you can look at the bigger circle of friends and others that you associate with. What does that look like? What kind of people do you have in your inner circle? Do you have a bunch of people who maybe look up to you and think you're smart and have leadership traits but don't particularly challenge your ideas and beliefs?

I consistently try to make sure I have a fairly eclectic group of friends, people I don't always agree with socially or politically but who are super smart and who can engage in a powerful, meaningful, and rational conversation without getting into petty bickering or name-calling. I try to avoid adding people to my crew who, when challenged with information that counters their beliefs, will proverbially throw their sucker down in the dirt, saying, "I'm not gonna talk to you anymore," take their ball, and go home.

One of my very good friends was a former Goldleaf employee of mine named Lee Wetherington. Lee may be the smartest person I know who is a contemporary of mine. Both Lee and I are fiscal conservatives. But politically, I consider myself a social libertarian and Lee would identify himself as socially liberal. As Lee reminds me, he is way more conservative with his own funds than I am with mine but, when it comes to the public's use of our tax dollars, I am probably more politically conservative than Lee is. We've worked extensively together, and we're now both professional speakers, so we talk a lot about the speaking business and delivery of financial services.

Over the years, we've had incredible conversations on topics I have seen other people get into knockdown, drag-out fights about. Lee and I have intelligent discussions, and we both take away a great deal of insight. I introduce him to certain elements or points of view, and he certainly does that for me. We both profit by the exchanges we have, even if neither of us change our opinions on a subject. I am truly blessed to have him as a friend.

If you're not looking for those kinds of people to include on your crew as friends, and if you're not expanding that crew to include people who will challenge you, then you have really done yourself a disservice. Only choosing people who think the way you do, who you can exert some kind of control and influence over, will only prevent you from growing. You want to find friends who say, "Hey, I have a different view, let me share my thoughts on this topic," and who aren't afraid to call you out on issues of importance.

Picking a crew can be viewed on four levels. First, at the senior management level, you're responsible for all or a significant portion of the employees of a company. Second, you're a supervisor of two to twelve employees. Third, you're an individual worker, but you have opportunities to put together cross-functional teams or something similar. Fourth, as an individual, you choose your spouse and friends. Who are the people you have chosen to be a part of your crew?

The Intangibles

As you consider hiring employees or acquiring friends, the intangibles of these individuals will make a critical difference. Think about the possible negative things that could happen over the period of time your crew will be together. If a crisis arises, what kinds of things would you perhaps need to do as a group in response? What kinds of skills would you want to have within the group in order to address the crisis? How will you assess whether or not the group you're assembling has all of those skills?

Let me give you an example. I booked a sailing charter in May of 2015 from Horizon Yacht Charters out of the British Virgin Islands. I've rented from them before, they're fantastic, and we had a wonderful time. However, halfway through our trip, we had a problem with our starboard engine. Of course, we didn't know what was wrong with the engine, but I didn't particularly care. All I did was pick up the direct cellphone back to Horizons and say, "Hey, there's a problem with this engine," and told them where we were. They arranged for somebody to come over and look at it and determined it was a water pump problem.

A mechanic cruised up in a boat with a new water pump and replaced it. Hey, we rented this sailboat, and that's their responsibility to do things like that. But, here's my point: one of our crew, Andy Wilkes, is the manager of a large plantation in South Georgia and, as a manager of a plantation, he has to know everything about all the different systems and equipment that a large plantation deploys. He knows all about equipment, and I'm convinced he can repair anything if he had duct tape and some bubblegum. He's involved in so many different things as a part of this plantation that he has extensive knowledge, including knowledge of diesel engine repair. He had already told me it was the water pump before they ever looked at it.

He said, "If you get me a water pump, I'll have that fixed for you."

I said, "Andy, that's not necessary. These guys will come and fix it."

Yet, if we had been sailing somewhere without access to Horizons to come and automatically fix it, I'm confident that Andy would have been able to fix that engine without any problem. His knowledge of diesel engines would have become critically important if we were sailing on a boat with a diesel engine out in the open ocean. Somebody on our crew or someone we could quickly access must have that knowledge.

Predicting Possible Crises

Being able to find people with multiple skill sets requires you to think ahead to the breadth of things that might happen in your company or life situation. What other kinds of skills should you be looking for?

A good example happened recently when I was involved in a mission trip from our church. In June of 2015, twenty-one people from our church traveled to a Christian campground located in LaFayette, Georgia, called The Family Center. As we advertised the mission project, we specifically asked for people who had particular skills related to the work we were being asked to do: carpentry, brush clearing, etc. We also knew there was a potential wallboard and mudding project, so we specifically asked, "Do you have experience with this? Is this something you can do?"

We found an individual who agreed to come and be a part of the mission team who specifically had that experience. We weren't completely sure we would need that skill because a different group had promised to have all of the wallboard for a newly constructed cabin completed before our arrival. Yet, the director of the camp told me this group had promised to get the project done for several months, but it was still uncompleted. When we arrived, sure enough, this other group had not been able to finish the project, so our crew with the experienced wallboard person completed that job.

We also had a nurse practitioner join our crew. There were two or three little injuries requiring her attention. It was especially helpful to have somebody with that kind of medical knowledge instead of having to take somebody to the hospital only to learn the situation was minor. In fact, one of the mission team members got some solvent in her eye, and we were able to deal with it using the medical expertise we had on the team, instead of having to take that person to the emergency room. (I should mention here that the nurse practitioner on our mission trip was my daughter, Kelly Spychalski, and I couldn't be more proud of her and her accomplishments).

Think about what your mission is, either from a business or personal standpoint, and start examining the kinds of negative things that could potentially happen, brainstorming Black Swan events. As a result of that brainstorming, you will come up with a list of possible crisis events. You can go further by asking, "If these events did happen, what should our response be? What skill sets would we need in order to respond in a way that mitigates the disaster?"

What should you be looking for in a potential new hire, both from a business standpoint and from a personal standpoint? Well, here is a list of attributes that I have found useful in examining any new potential hire (remember that any question you ask a potential employee should comply with all applicable state and federal laws):

Intangibles Skill List – Business

- Intelligence – Just raw smarts. Some really smart people can be a pain to work with but, generally, the smarter the better.

- Communication – I don't care how smart you are, if you cannot effectively communicate your ideas and thoughts, you are not of much value. Do they have any public speaking experience? Note: Public speaking is still one of the greatest fears that we have as humans. Each employee should be able to effectively communicate ideas in front of peers or customers.

- Leadership – Does the applicant show any leadership roles on the resume? Did they lead the band, chorus, or newspaper in high school? Did they lead projects at a previous company?

- Writing – Written communication is a bit of a lost art. Someone who can write a properly formatted email, especially in communications outside the company, is a big plus.

- Networking – Being able to connect with people and rally people to a cause.

- Stability under pressure – I hired a customer service manager who had done Unexploded Ordinance Disposal for the Air Force. This guy was not going to get rattled by an upset customer!

- Flexibility – Someone who sees change as an opportunity.

- Teamwork – Working together well in different group settings is very important.

- Multi-tasking – Okay, I understand that, technically, our brains do not "multitask." But can the candidate respond to the question, "How would you define multi-tasking, and how well do you accomplish it?"

- Positive attitude — Do they seem to be a generally upbeat positive person?

- Humility — Exhibits self-effacing behavior.

- Responsibility — Steps up and owns mistakes.

- Eagerness to learn new things / increase skill set — Show me someone who volunteers to take on a new task or skill, and I'll show you a future leader.

- Inspiration to others — Sometimes, a healthy work ethic speaks more than words.

- Encouragement to others — This may be hard to determine in the course of a typical business interview, but perhaps you could see how they respond to the question, "Describe the last time you were an encouragement to another individual or co-worker?"

- Fortitude — Shows perseverance through rough waters.

- Innovation — Ability to proverbially "think outside the box."

- Risk tolerance — People who are afraid to strike out never hit a homerun.

- Fallibility — The ability to fail and continue to innovate is perhaps the greatest underestimated intangible skill.

- Joie de vivre — (What, you don't speak French?) The "joy of life." I want people who are generally happy and upbeat.

Intangibles Skill List — Personal

- Intelligence — Again, the smarter the better, even if they're a pain to be a personal friend.

- Discretion — Can they keep a secret?

- Devil's Advocate — Are they willing to advocate for alternative positions?

- Ability to listen — Not pretend listen, really listen. "Give a short summary of what I just said," is a good test for this.

- Unselfish — Places the concerns of others first.

- Faithfulness — How loyal would they be in a tight situation?

- Integrity — Do they do the right thing even when no one is looking?

- Wisdom — Very different from intelligence, wisdom is the combination of experience and rational guidance that is exhibited in an appropriate way to the situation.

- Maturity — Do they act like a grown-up? (Note: There is a time and place for acting or playing like a child, so you don't have to be a grown-up all the time. But if you can't act like a grown-up when appropriate, you can't be my friend.)

After finding the required skills in a candidate, start looking at this "intangibles" list. What other skills does this person have that might meet the requirements to round out my team?

Assessing Skills

Don't forget to do a skill assessment of all your existing employees. Let's say you have thirty employees already, but over the next two years you're going to hire ten more. If you already know the intangible skills your existing employees have, you can compare them to the list at the end of the chapter and know where the gaps are. Your particular business might have a need for somebody with government relations experience or somebody who knows a little bit about the law or somebody who knows a little bit about social services work. This list will be different based on your particular business scenario and your individual strategic brainstorming about what skills might be necessary in a crisis for you or your organization.

Once you've compiled this list, have discovered the things you're looking for, and have conducted a skills assessment of what you already have, it becomes relatively straightforward for you to know what intangibles to look for as you hire new people.

As an example, let's go back to my time at Goldleaf. I had to hire a programmer. I had specific requirements for the programmer, but I also needed somebody with database skills. As I looked at candidates, the first thing I did was cull through the candidates, making sure they all met my minimum programmer requirements.

Out of that group, I had four candidates who all met those minimums. I interviewed all four of them. First and foremost, I checked whether or not they would fit on the team, how they would react and inter-react with everybody. Did they understand what our goals and values were, and did they fit in with those? I wanted to make sure they would be good team members first. Then, I wanted to know about their skills related to the minimum requirements as a programmer. I asked, "Explain to me how you meet or exceed all these skills." After I was satisfied about that, I looked at this list of ten other intangible skills and started asking them about their knowledge or expertise in those areas.

Two of the four candidates fit really well with the team and met all the minimum requirements as a programmer, but one of those two clearly stood out over the other in the intangibles. I let the intangibles swing my decision to hire that person. I've had situations when I was looking at three candidates who all would make good team members and who met the requirements. All of them had some of the intangibles. If there wasn't a clear choice, then I went back to some of the other areas, particularly the interaction with the other team members and those basic skills. If this person was a bit better than the other person in the basic skills, and they were equal in the intangibles, then I would let the superior basic skills swing the decision to that candidate.

Obscure Intangibles

What if a programmer also has a skill in something you would never consider useful, like flower arranging? You might say, "That would never be useful!"

Never say never. What about this scenario: let's say you're in a meeting with clients, partners, or vendors. There's usually a good bit of idle chitchat, casual conversation that goes back and forth. Now, all of a sudden, you find your employee and a prospect engaged in engrossing conversation about flower arranging. We can't say that flower arranging is a completely worthless skill. Hey, we have no idea when an obscure interest like that may be just the thing that connects a customer with an employee. Now, when you start the presentation, the customer is much more engaged because your employee made a personal connection with one of the attendees.

I will never say any intangible skill is of no use. But I will say this: in order for you to maximize the value of these intangible skills, you must do a strategic evaluation of the kinds of skills you're likely to need, not just in everyday operations but in the scenarios that, for you, would constitute a disaster.

If you're sailing, you know sails can rip. Who can take a needle and thread and repair sails? Engines fail. Who knows about diesel engines? You know there will be certain situations that could happen, unlikely perhaps, but possible. Who on board can handle that? If you were sailing to the island of Martinique, wouldn't it be a good idea to have somebody on board who spoke French? Of course!

Brainstorm what could possibly happen and assess the kinds of skills you would need. Then, take a skill assessment of yourself, all your chief lieutenants, and every member of your crew. Look for those skills your strategic analysis says you might need. Now you can see the gaps. "Hey, we don't have anybody who knows how to sew a sail." If I were a sailing captain hiring new sailors, I would not only look for people who can handle the lines and compass and read the stars, but I would also look for somebody who has experience in repairing a sail. I'm specifically looking for that. Whoever has that skill, all other basic sailing skills being equal, is probably going to become part of my crew.

You won't know if a candidate has intangibles unless you specifically ask about them. Of course, be sure you're not running afoul of the laws of your state or any federal laws regarding what kinds of questions you can ask potential employees. Within those parameters, ask your applicants (or your potential friends) specific questions. Ask them questions that give you information about whether or not they might have some of these skills. Or better, give them a little scenario that might represent a likely Black Swan event you have brainstormed. Ask them how they might be able to help in such a situation. This will not only tell you a lot about their intangible skills but also give you insight into their problem-solving acumen.

Once you start discovering who has which skill, then you need to keep track of these skill sets. How you will keep it up-to-date as your employees are acquiring additional skills? Are you, as a part of your education plan for employees, providing access to acquire additional skills? Let's say you're interviewing people, and there are two valuable skills you need, but they're not showing up in any of the applicants you have. Consider asking your current crewmembers, "Hey, would anybody be interested in taking some additional classes to learn about X? The company will pay for these classes." See who raises a hand. See who steps forward. Be sure to keep updating your list of crew members' known skills.

Making Difficult Decisions – Part 2

Let's return for a moment to the part of the *Grafton* story where Musgrave had to choose who of the crew would go in the dinghy for the sail to New Zealand. This is an interesting concept. Did Musgrave take Raynal because Raynal was close to him and had become a good friend? Did he think Raynal might have special insight if they ran into problems? Would Raynal have been able to do some repairs on the boat during the journey? Did he value Raynal's opinion, his ability to discuss ideas? Or had he formed such a close bond with him that he decided the two of them had to go together?

Then he chose Alick, the master seaman, as the next logical choice. When you're in a position to make choices about pulling together your team, then you have to do that based on some type of criteria. If you're in a leadership position, drawing straws rarely yields the best result. You pick specific team members for specific reasons. Now, this is different from a situation where you ask for volunteers. "Hey, we've got a project we want to do. Here are the criteria. Anybody who would like to volunteer for this and step up for this extracurricular activity, raise your hand." In that case, people self-select to be part of the group.

Usually when you're putting together a team, whether to deal with a crisis or to work on a project, you want that to be a cross-functional team. You must have specific people from specific areas of the company to be involved because you're tackling a certain problem. You look at the skill set of these different people and how they blend together. What kind of esprit de corps do they have? How well will they work together and interact with each other?

Training Others to Choose the Crew

If you're a senior leader, and you're trying to see how people below you exhibit leadership skills, then you should assign them a project where they're required to put together a team. Watch how they make the selection of that team. Let's say you need a project team, and it involves pulling together people from five different areas of the company. You've asked a middle manager to put this team together. Now, you observe. How does he make his selections?

His inclination might be to ask for volunteers, but you have instructed him on the importance of each of these team members; —they must have certain skills. In order to make sure you get those skills, you need to do an evaluation and pick the most qualified people to be on that team. As a senior leader, look at how he goes about making that decision. How does he exhibit leadership in pulling the team together? Probably the biggest single factor is whether or not he chooses the people who are his "peeps."

Does he grab his friends within the organization and put together a team of buddies regardless of whether those individuals meet the skill set needed? Or does he look for the people who have the specific skills, who might even exhibit other skills outside of the specific required skill, because he thinks these people are super smart or experienced? Does he look for people who can collaborate even if they might otherwise be socially difficult to be around?

That's a good way to get an idea about how a potential rising star exhibits leadership skills and decision-making esprit de corps.

Give him opportunities to make decisions and exhibit leadership in non-crisis situations.

As he builds that team, you sit down and discuss the process with him. "Okay, Jones, explain to me why you picked these five. I see you picked Johnson from accounting. Why not Smith? Why did you choose Johnson over Smith?"

Maybe he responds, "Well, I've had a lot of interaction with Johnson. I'm pretty familiar with him."

"Yeah, but did you look into the background of Smith and know that she actually ran her own company and that experience would be valuable and specifically relevant to this particular project?"

Encouraging Great Team Formation

You're not trying to slam Jones for his decisions. You're trying to help him understand how making those decisions might affect the overall project. One of the biggest problems in many organizations is a lack of leadership training, growing people up to become leaders. An up-and-coming leader must understand if he or she is buddies with everyone and then becomes a leader, it's very difficult to lead and remain everybody's friend.

At the end of the day, you have to be their leader, and you have to exhibit leadership over friendship. Sometimes that means making tough decisions, perhaps even picking a team member over somebody who is a close friend. When you have this opportunity to give people the chance to make leadership decisions about how they might pull a group together, it gives you that chance to offer learning lessons. Guide them to understand the kind of decisions they make and whether those are being made based on friendship or camaraderie as opposed to an objective look at the skill set needed.

One other benefit of leadership training is that those people within your organization who aren't socially mingling with others, who may be generally ostracized, will be more likely considered for a team. By making sure that people who have skills get pulled into teams, you also are helping them become more active. You're putting them in a situation where they have to collaborate with others, especially if they're in a technical field.

Some employees like to go into their own little world where it's dark, and you could grow mushrooms. They want to sit and work all day and not interact with people. Get those people who are less social and less likely to participate involved in collaborative events, so they can grow team skills.

Misrepresented Skills

What kinds of skills assessments might be done on an ongoing basis? Suppose you've done a great job of assessing skills and looking for the intangibles. You've factored in everything and hired somebody, but as the new employee begins working, and you have a chance to see him interact beyond the interview, you realize you've misread some of the characteristics you saw in him. Maybe you thought he was going to be a great team player, but he's a loner. Maybe you asked some questions about intangibles and misread his responses.

Or perhaps he intentionally misled you, stating he had certain skills and abilities but clearly doesn't. Certainly, you'd have to seriously question anybody who misrepresents his skills and abilities. What else is he not being truthful about? What do you do about that? If the employee has misrepresented a required skill— if he said he knows the Python programming language, but it's evident after ninety days that he knows more about "Monty Python" than Python programming—then you have a responsibility to do something about that.

You can't allow a person's lack of skill to add to the burden of the other employees. Think about what message you are sending to the rest of your employees about how you value them. You can't allow somebody who is obviously substandard on required skills to stay. You say, "Hey, you told me you could do this, and you can't. You have to go."

The intangible skills are a little bit different. If a candidate falsely claims he or she has some of these intangible skills, but he or she is very good at the primary skills, you wouldn't say, "You told me you knew how to work on diesel engines, so even though you're an expert sailor (and we might never need you to work on diesel engines), you misrepresented yourself about this skill. Get out." That doesn't make sense to me.

First, determine whether or not somebody intentionally misled you. Was this person trying to obfuscate or overstate their capabilities? Or was it just a misunderstanding? Maybe it was the way you asked the questions. Have an honest conversation:

"Hey, I asked these questions, and your responses gave the impression you had this skill."

"Oh, no. I'm so sorry. I thought you were talking about X, and here's where my skills actually are."

Sometimes, it can be just an honest misunderstanding. I think, far too often in business and in our personal lives, we jump to conclusions about what someone said rather than simply asking, "Hey, this is what I thought we were talking about. What did you think we were talking about?" Make sure you get on the same page.

Suppose you hired an employee who's doing a great job as a programmer. He did not intentionally mislead you, but he's not as strong in one of those intangibles (say database management) as you thought. Cutting him loose doesn't make a lot of sense. Remember, you hired him for the primary skill (and by my own admission, in this example, he's doing a great job in that primary skill). This is where you need to say, "Hey, I need you to be more knowledgeable in database management, so I want you to acquire this skill outside of all the other duties you have. The company will pay you to attend this school or take this online class, but you have to do this on your own time. So, do all your regular tasks as well as take this class because this is a skill set we want you to have. It's important for the team."

You have the opportunity in those situations to make an honest evaluation of people who turn out to be less skilled than you thought or perhaps were disingenuous in how they represented their skills. As early as you can in the process, if it becomes necessary, cut them loose. I can think of many situations when I left somebody in a position who wasn't quite making it, because I said, "Well, I need somebody in that position. Later, I'll try to find somebody else."

In general, putting off the inevitable creates more problems. Whatever burden of extra work you temporarily place on the other employees by getting rid of the employee who clearly isn't cutting it will have a lesser negative impact than keeping somebody who's obviously not making it. In that case, the other employees have the extra burden anyway, and they have to deal with this person every day, knowing he is not carrying his weight.

In general, employees recognize and applaud a manager who says, "I'm firing this person because it's important that everyone on this team pull his own weight. This person was clearly not pulling his own weight. I'm letting him go, and I'm getting a suitable replacement." You may have to keep somebody on for a period of time and overlap, but, in general, I think you will see great benefit in the appreciation of the other employees when you refuse to keep somebody past the point you become aware they are completely ineffective or subpar team members. The esprit de corps will grow. Your team will band together, rise up, and do the extra work, knowing you had their backs by getting rid of somebody who was a burden to the team.

Nobody likes to fire employees. Well, I guess that's not true. I'm sure there are people who like to fire employees, but hopefully you don't have any managers who enjoy firing people. Sometimes you have to do it, and you need to do it as professionally as possible. Quite frankly, both you and the employee deserve to get it over with as quickly as possible when you know it's not going to work out.

Intangible Skills Assessment

All other things being equal, choose the candidate with the most diverse skill set. Captain Musgrave of the *Grafton* never got to mine the ore he originally sought. He and the crew went in search of seals and wound up shipwrecked on Auckland Island. But, he had the forethought to select François Raynal as first mate. Raynal was so intelligent and skilled, he did the following things that had nothing to do with sailing and mining ore, but wound up being critical to their comfort, attitude, and ultimate survival:

- He made soap – critical to their mental well-being, staying clean.

- He made clothes – after several months, their original clothes were in tatters.

- He created tools – used to cook, hunt, and ultimately, make a seaworthy sailboat out of the dinghy.

- He made distilled spirits – but realized the danger and threw it out, claiming he had failed.

- He made cement – necessary to hold the stones together for the fireplace/chimney.

- He created a forge – yes, a real forge, on a deserted island in the South Pacific.

The forge – a marvel considering the limited resources
—Alfred De Neuville Engraving, Public Domain—

- He was a motivator and encouraged the others, but was a particular encouragement to Captain Musgrave.

- He was a counselor to Musgrave, providing a critically important sounding board for Musgrave to bounce ideas around with.

- He brought ideas and suggestions to Musgrave – it was actually Raynal who first suggested the election of a leader.

Enough intangibles? Don't you want Raynal on your team?

CHAPTER SEVEN
Seeking Advice

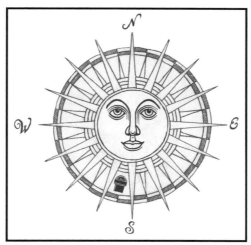

"Not all those who wander are lost."

— J.R.R. Tolkien,
The Fellowship of the Ring

After more than four hours of sailing, we had seen nothing but water, endless water in every direction. We saw nothing that would indicate we were even close to land—a bird, a floating coconut. While there was not much conversation about our situation, we were all thinking, "This cannot be right. We should have seen the

Bahamas." Then we spotted something on the horizon ... another boat, a motor cruiser, headed across our path in a southwesterly direction!

Without knowing what radio channel they were monitoring and knowing that, at the speed they were traveling, we only had a short window to hail them, we shot off a flare and blasted our air horn. They spotted us, slowed, and redirected to come near our sailboat. It was a group of men on a fishing trip.

We exchanged pleasantries and asked, "Can you help us fix our position? We think if we keep heading on a northeasterly course, 045 on the compass, we should reach West End, Bahamas."

They quizzically looked at each other, looked toward the northeast, and one of them said, "If you keep going that way, the next thing you'll hit is England! The Bahamas are back that way." He pointed in the direction they were headed. No way! They got the chart out, showed us where we were, well northeast of West End, and helped us determine the compass setting that would take us there. We checked our compass against theirs and confirmed that it was giving the same reading. They gave us ice and some cold drinks and then sped off. Armed with this new information, we followed them, and, for a few minutes, we could see the evidence of their trail. We were confident we were finally on the right track.

So, you've set a new course, and you're taking different readings along the way to make sure you're on the right course. But, at some point, it may become necessary to look outside of yourself or your organization and find some independent advice. You might automatically think that getting any advice in a crisis situation is probably always good, but the quality of the advice and the trustworthiness of the source really matters.

Finding the Right Source

Obviously, there are different types of advice. At the most basic level, there's good advice and bad advice. If you reach out to somebody who gives bad advice, that's not helpful. Even if you ultimately recognize it as bad advice and don't act on it, the time you spent acquiring it was wasted. Getting advice has to start with a frame of reference concerning whether or not the individual or entity to whom you are seeking advice is trustworthy. Is this a reliable source of advice?

But if you are in the middle of a crisis, how do you know what source of information is trustworthy? Of course, planning for a disaster before it occurs provides you the luxury of vetting sources for trustworthiness.

Let me return to Goldleaf and the software problem we were experiencing. I could have done some things to lessen the impact of the systemic slowdown of the service. I knew I was dealing with certain programming languages, operating systems, and database structures. There was a list of things most likely involved if a problem came up with the software. Now, all of a sudden, my company was in a moment of crisis, and I'm trying to figure out, "Who are we going to call? Who are the experts in these systems?"

But, I had a problem. I had not taken the time to cultivate a resource list that would catalog experts for each of the systems we were using. If I had a database problem, here's the database expert I would contact and a backup to that expert, and so on down the line. Without time pressure, you can do a thorough job ensuring each of these resources is reliable and trustworthy. But what happens when you are in the midst of a disaster, and you are looking for outside help. How can you vet a source for trustworthiness?

Confident and Decent Sources

Say you were in a large, unfamiliar city, looking for the train station. You're late and urgently need to find the station to make your train. You stop and ask someone, "Can you tell me where the train station is?"

They say, "Sure, go four blocks that way and turn right for two more blocks, and you're there."

Okay, so off you go.

Two elements likely subconsciously registered in your brain. One, this person was confident in giving the directions, an indication that she had the requisite knowledge to answer your question. Two, there was no reason to believe she would respond in a dishonest way.

Suppose in the same example, the person to whom you asked directions had said, "Well, I think it's over near the convention center. I would say head four blocks in that direction and then it's a couple of blocks more to the right."

That sounds a bit sketchier. You quickly determine that, perhaps, she isn't sure of where the station is, and you either discard her advice altogether and look for another reliable source, or you might head in the direction she suggested but immediately look for additional information to confirm the directions. In either case, you have no reason to believe she would purposely give you bad information.

Consider another scenario. You take a cab, but it was a less than pleasant experience. So, when you reach your destination, you pay the cabbie, but do not add a tip. Then you ask for directions. The cab driver gives you directions and off you go. But the directions turn out to be bad. Did he purposefully give you wrong directions based on you not tipping? In this scenario, there is a plausible reason for him to purposefully offer untrustworthy advice.

How does this relate to our situation aboard the *Alacrity*? We had sailed in a northeasterly course, thinking we were headed toward

West End, and we had a firm belief we were on the right track. We were out in the middle of the Atlantic Ocean and were not seeing any land. We weren't getting any confirmation whatsoever that we were on the right track. Very discouraging.

Now, all of a sudden, we see a boat! This boat was moving fast. We have a limited amount of time to make some kind of contact. Think about this: the ocean is a massive place; it's not like an interstate where you're passing cars all the time. Out on the open ocean, you can go for a long time, days or weeks even, and not see another vessel. Actually seeing another vessel is a rare occurrence. Not only was it unusual that we saw this boat, but it could have been a few miles away on either side of our track, and we wouldn't have seen it at all.

We were desperate to get some new information on our position, so we shot off a flare gun and diverted their attention to come over to speak with us. We explained the situation—here is where we thought we were, this is where we're trying to go, and we think if we continue going in this northeasterly direction we'll hit West End.

Their reaction was swift and immediate: "No. The only thing that's in that direction is England, a good distance away. We are actually headed to West End, and it's back the other way, behind you." We had them get their chart and compared it with ours, confirmed where our position was, and checked our instrumentation. We were convinced the information they were giving us was correct. But, actually, we had little choice, as there were no other options for accessing new information.

It's possible they could have given us false information. We were probably ready to believe anything they told us. But they were nice, reasonable sounding people. They gave no indication they were unsure of their opinion. There was no reason for them to be untruthful with us. Boaters out on the water are generally completely open to share in situations such as ours, and go out of their way to help other boaters who are in need. The key here is that we were in a position where we needed to get additional information and, luckily for us, by the providence of God actually, these boaters came by who had the information we needed in order to accurately fix our position.

We moved from an assumption (or a misinterpreted fact) of where we were to a reasonable fact of where we were, and now we could set a new course and move toward our destination. Ultimately, in this case, it turned out that information was correct. We did, in fact, get to West End later that day.

Don't Accept Information at Face Value out of Desperation

Here's an important point: we were desperate. They could have told us we needed to go due east at that point. I wonder sometimes what would have happened if we had come across people who were less honorable. They could have robbed us, killed us, and stolen our sailboat. Or they could have just made up a story, "Hey, you're here on the chart. Head directly east."

They could have told us almost anything, and we probably would have believed them. But even in our desperation for new information, we took the time to look at charts, to confirm compass settings, to confirm what they were telling us was true.

I strongly caution you: when you get desperate, when you get to the point where you're willing to accept any information as gospel truth, you need some mechanism, some way, to verify to yourself that it's actually correct. Are you so desperate that you're willing to take what anybody may say and run with it as the truth without it passing the sniff test? If you weren't in a crisis situation, would you assess this information and not give it any credibility? You have to look further at the source of the new information and whether or not the source is reliable regardless of their ability to provide additional information in this one instance.

Here are some questions that can assist you in making this determination:

- Does this source of information have any reason to be untruthful?

- Do I have any evidence that this source has been untruthful in the past?

- How confidently is the source relaying information? Are they extremely sure, somewhat sure, or just guessing at a response?

- What can be immediately verified about the information to gauge its veracity?

- Given the time pressure, do I have any way of accessing another source of information to verify what I am being told?

Make your best effort to determine how reliable the information is. Then, base your actions on information you can reasonably determine is reliable. When information is determined to be unreliable, stop, reassess, and take a new course of action.

The Unencumbered Outsider

Maybe you've experienced something similar. Something comes up, like a software bug (or whatever is applicable in your world or industry). You immediately redirect your people, who are experts in your code, to the problem. That's what we did the day of the slowdown. Then, the next day, you're still looking through it and can't figure it out. Then, it happens the next week, and you still can't figure it out. Maybe you continue for a long period of time, trying to fix the problem.

On Monday, when it happened for the second time in three days, as the senior executive of this company, I should have said, "Hey, wait a minute. If we don't really know or understand this issue, if we can't immediately put our finger on what this is, let's think about all the different things that it could be, even those that are kinda crazy, out of left field."

To do that properly, you most likely need to bring in somebody from the outside to take a good, hard look at what's happening. A qualified outside consultant doesn't have the benefit of knowing everything about your code. You might say, "Why would I want somebody who's not knowledgeable about my code?"

The knowledge of the code and the familiarity with the system can also be a detriment. Your staff, particularly those that created the systems, can be overconfident of what something cannot be. You've probably heard someone in your organization say, "Well, it can't be that." That's a great example of the automated thinking I referenced in Chapter 1.

Really? How do you know it can't be that? When you bring in somebody from the outside, they look at the facts and say what they think it might be based on their experience and independent observation. Then, you can chase down those things. Because we were so convinced we were the experts in this area, and we would be the ones to identify what the anomaly was, we let a lot of time go by. Instead, we should have a) more immediately identified that we had a Black Swan and b) brought somebody in from outside our organization from the very beginning who could have looked at everything as it was.

Let me highlight two interesting points before we close this chapter. Based on the sextant reading, we determined we were south and west of West End.

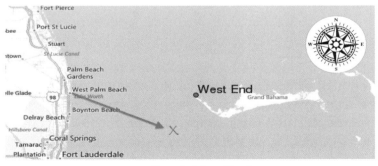

—Google Maps/Earth

Suppose we had decided to head west to return to the United States. We would have sighted Florida somewhere well south of our home port of West Palm Beach, maybe south of Boca Raton, maybe Pompano Beach or Ft. Lauderdale, somewhere south of where we thought we were. If we had turned around and gone west from where we actually were, we would have wound up being well north of our home port, maybe Ft. Pierce or even Daytona Beach.

Imagine, if you will, that you are with us aboard the *Alacrity*. The sun comes up. All we see is water. No land in sight! We take a sextant reading. "Oh, my gosh! Look at how far south and west we really are. Hey, you know what? Let's just head west. We'll wind up somewhere in Boca Raton, then just sail north to get to our house."

So, we sail for a number of hours and, boom, there's Florida right there. But, that doesn't look like Boca Raton. "Holy cow! That's not Boca Raton. That's Daytona Beach!" We're a hundred miles or more north of where we thought we were. Then, we turn around and head south. My point here is that we wouldn't find the Florida coast and immediately start sailing north to get to West Palm Beach. We would find the Florida coast and use landmarks to know exactly where we were on that coast. Then, make the necessary course correction from there.

Also, consider this. We were in the Atlantic Ocean, heading for where we thought West End, Bahamas should be. We saw this boat and received new information, affixing a new, correct position. Before we started sailing southwest toward West End, we could have taken another sextant reading right then. Doing so would have allowed us to compare where the sextant said we were to where the fishing boat crew said we were.

Why do that? Either the sextant wasn't working correctly, or we weren't using it correctly. Assuming the new position was a fact, we could have determined how to use the sextant to give us the correct position. That would have made the sextant a more reliable source of information for any future use of it to affix a position. When you have the opportunity to confirm process-es and procedures in a time of calm to cement your knowledge of how to use tools to provide reliable information, take full advantage.

CHAPTER EIGHT

The Destination

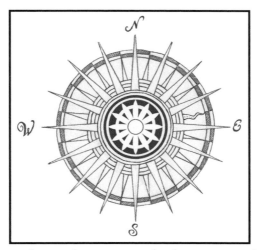

*"We are free to choose our paths, but we can't choose
the consequences that come with them."*

— Sean Covey

When you ask people about strategy, many will offer catchphrases. If you ask the typical community bank executive about strategy for their organization, he might say, "We will provide superior personalized customer service." Such common buzzwords! Is this really a differentiator between financial institutions?

David Faulkner, the CEO of Next Branch Strategies, recently did an analysis of all the financial institutions near a bank wanting to transform their retail branches. He specifically looked for competitors' brand value statements, in essence, their strategic direction. Of the twelve financial institutions in the same market, there was literally no difference in what they advocated as strategic direction on their websites: Great Customer Service! Personalized Attention! We Put You First!

You have likely seen ads and messaging from banks along these lines. I don't even agree that providing good customer service is a strategic direction. I, and many others who think and write about strategic direction, agree there are shockingly few companies that truly have a strategic direction.

One of these writers is Ron Shevlin, who is a Gonzobanker at Cornerstone Advisors. Ron is a voracious market researcher, researching concepts and trends in the financial services sector. I find his writing insightful because he provides a wealth of thought-provoking information in a snarky and fun way. He takes an honest, introspective look at the things most of us gloss over.

Recently, he wrote a blog post about this idea of strategy. In it, he mentioned a study that revealed fifty percent of employees don't know their company's strategy. One opinion offered for the reason they didn't know the strategy was that the senior manager, let's say the CEO, didn't necessarily want the employees to know the strategy because, wait for it, they couldn't be trusted with that information. It might fall into the hands of competitors.

While there may be some truth to that (I mean, obviously companies do not want to see their strategy get in the hands of competitors), I think the more accurate reason, and the one Ron offers in this blog, is they don't have a strategy. The reason that fifty percent of the employees don't know the strategy is because no one in the company knows the strategy. Therefore, it can't be imparted. If, in fact, senior management doesn't know what the strategy is, then certainly the other employees won't know it. It makes you wonder what the fifty percent of the employees who say they know the strategy are working to achieve.

Is It the Right Direction?

Also consider whether your strategic direction is well-conceived, reasonable, and likely to be successful. Captain Musgrave and Raynal of the *Grafton* had been talking to two benefactors. One of them, Charles Sarpy, Raynal already knew, and the other one was Musgrave's uncle. Musgrave and Raynal simply wanted to make their fortunes. Raynal had been a prospector for ten years, searching for gold, and was an engineer before that. Musgrave was a master mariner from England. He had been a captain since the age of sixteen, sailing many different vessels before deciding to settle down in Sydney, where he regularly sailed back and forth between Australia and New Zealand. That job ended.

At that point, both men were eager to make some serious money. Uncle Musgrave and Charles Sarpy told them that Campbell Island had argentiferous tin. When Musgrave and Raynal heard "argentiferous" come out of these men's lips, they became enthralled with the idea of seeking this treasure.

As you read through Joan Druett's well-researched book, *Island of the Lost*, it becomes clear there was some sketchiness about this particular venture from the beginning. Campbell Island was a volcanic rock island dissected by glaciers. So, while it was remotely possible that it was a source of argentiferous tin, Raynal, with his experience, perhaps should have known that the chances did not warrant the trip. Moreover, Campbell Island is a harsh, remote area with a hostile climate. The available charts showing safe anchorages were primitive, but even those primitive charts clearly indicated the whole area was dangerous to navigate. There were few places where you could safely anchor. Not only that, but there were also many sailors in the Sydney area who knew the sub-Antarctic region well and provided warnings about just how hostile it was.

Keep Your Head About Ya

Let's consider some things. First of all, Raynal should have had enough experience to evaluate all the information the two investors gave him. He should have been able to figure out that this could likely be a fool's errand. One of the points Joan Druett makes is that the word "argentiferous" and the possibility they would become wildly rich overcame all reasonable objections.

She states, "Because of that one enticing word, they had agreed to go along with a scheme that more sensible men would have turned down without hesitation" (Druett 5). Even though these men exercised a significant amount of logic, reasoning, leadership, and positive decision-making after the wreck, the fact that they actually took on this adventure shows their original plan was flawed from the very start.

Had they sat down and asked a series of questions about what the risks were? "What is the best outcome we could achieve? What are the likely negative outcomes we must consider? What could we possibly come back with? What is the realistic chance for success? What facts do we have that would indicate that the ore we seek is actually on this island?"

If they had asked more probing questions, perhaps they would have looked at this voyage in a totally different light and maybe determined the venture was not likely to succeed.

What You Won't Do

Another important concept relative to determining your strategy that Ron Shevlin raises, which is both relevant to our discussion and counter-intuitive, is to decide what you will not do. Think about that for a moment. You generally don't go around saying, "Well, here are all the things we're not going to do." It's easier to say what you are going to do. But, sometimes people have a clearer understanding about what they won't do.

This approach sets some riverbanks through which they can navigate and find success. Knowing you have a limited amount of resources and an idea of what those resources are might dictate certain things you'd like to do, but it will absolutely dictate things that you can't or won't do. Think about the ships, how they were outfitted, how their crews were hired, and so on. There were certain expeditions they wouldn't have attempted based on the type of ship they had, the size of the ship they had, and the type of crew they had.

So, know what you won't do and don't make exceptions for any activity that is on your "no" list. Make sure that information gets imparted to your crew, partners, and customers. Likewise, it's important to ask questions when you are interviewing with a company for employment. It's fair for you to ask probing questions about their strategy and business practices, in a professional way, so you can understand a company's strategy and what they won't do.

Limiting Opportunities Can Increase Sales?

Let me give you a couple of examples of deciding what you won't do. From the start of Goldleaf, I made a decision that we would create and sell software only to financial institutions. They wouldn't have to get a loan in order to buy software, and they always paid their bills on time. Next, I decided I would only sell to banks where I could get the President/CEO on the phone, meaning, once the bank was too big that the CEO wouldn't take my call, they were too big to be our customer.

Now, as you can imagine, this limited us in getting some big deals with larger US-based financial institutions. Yet at that time and through my own experience, I knew the larger institutions had more red tape and more approval steps necessary to finish a deal. Goldleaf had selling cycles of a few weeks; a large financial institution could take up to two years to make a decision.

Based on the size of our nascent company, even if they wanted to purchase our software, they might elect not to do so, thinking that we were too small to be considered a vendor for them. I was not willing to waste our valuable and scant resources chasing big opportunities that may never close. We stuck to community banks and credit unions. And in fifteen years, we signed over 2,500 institutions that bought at least one of our software modules or web-based services.

In the early days after we created Goldleaf, we had an opportunity to do some business with correspondent banks. For those unfamiliar with the banking lexicon, a correspondent bank is a bank that has other banks as customers. We were working with a banker's bank in Florida, and ultimately sold them (and other banker's banks) a software package that allowed for the automation of financial transactions. Because it was a PC-based system, there was some interest in it from the country of Panama, and we installed it there.

In the ensuing years, we also installed it in Aruba and in Trinidad-Tobago. They didn't need or want the expense of a large mainframe computer system, and we had a software product that not only provided correspondent automation but also had all of the net settlements to do clearing transactions between financial institutions, very much like the Federal Reserve does here in the United States. That product was called GOLDNet.

We then had the opportunity to expand our reach in the Caribbean and Latin America. We started garnering more inquiries from Africa and Europe. We even received inquiries from some countries in Asia wanting us to come there and talk to them about selling GOLDNet.

Is It Worth It?

At the time, I thought through these opportunities.

One, we were a small company. Were we going to run all around the world chasing this? If we sold one, we would have to go service it halfway around the world. Were we going to travel regularly to those countries?

Two, as I looked at some of these countries, they were less likely to be enthralled with our product at the time. Remember, we're talking about 1995–1998 and even into 2000. The explosion of networks and cloud computing didn't exist. The larger the country, the more likely they were using mainframes or systems like the IBM AS/400. Our system wasn't like that and wasn't going to be that. I saw the possibility of us going over there, presenting the product to them, getting them excited about it, but hearing them say, "Oh, wait a minute. GOLDNet runs on microcomputers. It's running on MS-DOS. Can you port this over to the AS/400?"

The countries we were already involved in were so close. We could fly to Miami and, from there, have quick access to pretty much anywhere in Latin America and the Caribbean. Since we were already successful in one region, and we didn't want to overextend ourselves, I made the decision that we would not chase any of these other opportunities.

Before that final decision was made, Ben Jordan, our most senior business development officer, a super smart, super sharp advocate for our product, did go over to Nigeria and was part of a presentation over there. But while he was there, he had to have an armed guard with him at all times for safety.

I thought, "You know what? That is just not worth it." I worried the whole time he was over there, and didn't breathe a sigh of relief until he was back in the United States.

We said, "That's it. No."

That Nigeria presentation was enough to confirm for me that we did not need to go outside our region. We stayed within the Caribbean and Latin America. We even refused some opportunities in South America, not because of the distance so much but because they did not trust a PC-based product.

So, as you make decisions and determine what you're not going to do, you are forming a strategy. You may not think of it as a strategy, but by defining what you won't do, you have reduced the number of things that you will do, and it helps get you where you want to be.

The Backup Plan

Suppose you have a strategy and, for reasons outside your control, it is not working out to be a beneficial, profitable strategy. What's your backup plan? Don't have one? This is common.

Creating a backup plan right away might seem to some as if you are not totally committed to the original strategy. But thinking about a backup strategy up front has the benefits of allowing you to select crew and equipment that would be suitable for multiple potential destinations.

Returning to the story of the *Grafton*, Musgrave and Raynal had the original intention of finding silver-bearing ore on Campbell Island. So, they went and searched, but it was not there. However, they had already planned as a part of their strategy that if they failed to locate the ore, they would instead hunt and process seals. Seal hunting was a completely viable alternative activity for generating revenue in the 1860s.

As it turned out, not only was there no silver-bearing ore, there weren't any seals on Campbell Island either, so they went to Auckland Island. Everybody on the *Grafton* knew that seal hunting was potentially a part of their ultimate strategic direction. We don't have access to the details surrounding the mission of the *Invercauld*, other than the fact that they were headed to South America to get a load of fertilizer. We will never know if there was an alternate plan, but everybody on that ship knew they were going after fertilizer.

The *Grafton* had an alternate plan because they knew the benefactors back in Australia, who were funding the whole operation, wanted a return on the investment. They thought, "Look, we're not going to come back empty-handed. We're going to come back with something, so we can pay for this trip and make money for ourselves and our benefactors."

Articulating Strategic Direction

From a leadership standpoint, you should know your strategic direction. Shevlin's article on strategy mentions the possibility that the only job you have as a CEO would be to brainstorm the answers to the following seven questions and be able to articulate the answers effectively:

1. What is our current strategy?

2. Is our current strategy working?

3. If it's not, what should our new strategy be?

4. How should it be different from the old one?

5. What are we going to do now?

6. How do I communicate that strategy, so we don't have mass mutiny?

7. How do we execute on the strategy?

If you're a business leader, if you manage people, or if you're in a position of making decisions, and you can't answer those seven questions, especially articulating the strategy to the relevant stakeholders, there's a problem. Let me skinny Ron's seven questions down to just three.

1. Is our current strategy working? Yes/No.

2. If we answer "No," what's the new strategy, and how's it going to be different from the other one?

3. If "Yes," how do we effectively communicate this to all stakeholders?

Let's examine it as a programming decision tree:

Even If you answer, "Yes, it's working," then you still need to answer these questions: How am I communicating that strategy? How am I executing the strategy?

Discovering Your Personal Strategic Direction

I want to also address strategic direction for individuals. If you are not a business owner or a senior manager, how does all this apply to you? You need to spend time in deep introspection about your strategic direction. You might have a deeply held desire, something you wanted to do with your life. Perhaps as a young child, you might have wanted to be a veterinarian, astronaut, or fireman.

There could be something in you, a desire that compels you to pursue a particular career or activity that you've never been able to explore before. Maybe you've never taken steps to make this dream happen. Some people look at different career options from the perspective of what economic gain they could make from that job. Most people want to achieve certain milestones: marry, have a family, and buy a house. These represent certain economic realities.

Sometimes I think about my fly fishing guide friends out in Colorado, and I think, "What a life those guys have!" However, most of them also work two or three other jobs, particularly in the off-season to make ends meet because being a fly fishing guide is not exactly a lucrative activity.

In choosing a career, you consider the economic side as well as personal enjoyment. Since her early years, my daughter, Kelly, liked animals and wanted to become a veterinarian. I told her, "Hey, I'm fully supportive of that, but just think about this. The need for veterinarians is out there, but if you become a people medical person, if you become a doctor or nurse or something like that, your options for employment will be significantly higher. Your love for animals and your ability to care for animals will always be there, even if you work in a human medical field."

She not only had the desire to pursue nursing, but she's also adept at it and is now a nurse practitioner, working in Ohio and doing extremely well. That's not to say she couldn't have been an outstanding veterinarian, but her career options as a medical practitioner now are extremely broad compared to veterinary services. As the populations of the world age, the health care workers and people who can do what she does will be even more important, so she can pretty much go anywhere in the world and there will be a well-paying job for somebody with her kind of skills.

What about your life-long dream? What's the bottom line—your passion (or your income, your financial stability, or your financial success)?

Pivot Slightly

Once you start setting some boundaries and learning what you would do and what you wouldn't do, then you can look for a job you know you like. Suppose a job opportunity comes along that is similar but different from what you were seeking? Perhaps it's a slight pivot from your perceived sweet spot, and you are not sure if it will work out. If you ascertain that the new opportunity has enough of the attributes you already know appeal to you and work to your strengths, you can know the opportunity is worth pursuing.

Maybe the new opportunity is in an innovative and exciting field, not exactly what you're seeking, but close. How do you make the decision? You either say, "No, no. I'm going to stay put" or "Yes, I'm going for the new opportunity." This is another important aspect of determining strategic direction both for individuals and for businesses. Let me share another Goldleaf example.

In the early 2000s, the Automated Clearing House (ACH) created a check conversion option. You could take a physical, paper check and convert it into an ACH payment, an electronic transaction that went through the payment system. The image wasn't delivered, but the detail of the check would show up on your monthly statement with the check number and the amount. Because Goldleaf was an ACH vendor, and our job was to enable whatever type of ACH transactions were permissible, we added the ability to incorporate scanners into our web-based application. We were one of the first vendors to have this scanning capability out there for ACH.

Ultimately, through mismanagement of the ACH rules, those check conversion transactions never reached the potential they could have. Nevertheless, that capability existed in our software, and we sold a lot of software to community financial institutions to capitalize on that opportunity. In 2003, a law passed called Checking for the 21st Century, a result of the 9/11 catastrophe. When the planes stopped flying that day, the checks that flew around in the bellies of planes stopped moving. That became the impetus for the industry to say, "Why aren't we converting paper checks into digital images?" In October of 2004, Checking for the 21st Century finally became active, which meant the image of a check would carry the same legal weight as a paper check.

Because Goldleaf already had scanning software for the conversion of checks into ACH, it was fairly straightforward to create a modification of the program that allowed the same kind of scanning of checks to make this new "Check 21"check image file. We did that and had our first live installation in January 2005. We sold that software to hundreds of banks because we were able to pivot quickly, modifying the check capture technology we already had.

Earlier in this chapter I talked about what we wouldn't do at Goldleaf: run all over Europe, Asia, and Africa with GOLDNet. And here's an example of what we would do: take something already in our wheelhouse (creating and processing ACH and related payment transactions for community financial institutions), capitalize on the Check 21 opportunity to be nearly the first to market, and get a great deal of market share in the process. Both ideas are relevant for a business owner or senior manager who's trying to make these kinds of strategic decisions, but it's also critically important that we think about our strategic direction as individuals.

When something new comes along, a brand new opportunity that could wind up being very rewarding, possibly financially lucrative, does your skill set allow you to pivot and attempt the new thing? Does this opportunity align with your competencies, and is there a reasonable likelihood of future success? If so, seriously consider including it in your individual strategic direction.

Strategic Direction Leads to Strategic Destination

At the end of the day, you have to know what your strategic direction is. If you don't know that, then you don't know if your ship is adequate, you don't know if the crew is trained, and you don't know if your plan is going to work. You just sort of wind up somewhere. By having a definitive, strategic direction, you are more likely to arrive at your specific strategic destination.

Along the way, continue asking the three questions:

Is my current strategy working? Yes/No.

If I answer "No," what's my new strategy, and how's it going to be different from the other one?

If "Yes," how do I effectively communicate this to all stakeholders?

If the strategy is not working, be prepared to change the strategy and move toward something else, a new opportunity, the equivalent of saying, "Hey, there's no tin ore on Campbell Island. We're going to Auckland Island to hunt seals." You prepare the ship and crew for that alternative activity. What changes do you need to make today to reach your specific strategic goals?

Becoming the Captain

Maybe you don't work at an exciting business but are thinking of starting one. As someone who has started numerous ventures, I am often asked what process I use to determine the type of company I would create. There are no hard and fast rules. I would certainly not put up my accomplishments in comparison to people like Steve Jobs, Bill Gates, or Richard Branson, but I have had a level of success. There are questions I ask myself regarding starting a new enterprise.

What are my areas of expertise? Creating a new venture in an area where you have limited or no experience is more risky.

What do my target customers want to buy? There are way too many examples of solutions that were created in search of a problem.

Do I have insight or information that would give me an edge over potential competitors? If you know a certain law or regulation is going to create an opportunity, are you able to capitalize on that before anyone else?

Do I have the people, budget, and tools needed to create this business (or alternatively, to add this product or service to my existing business)?

This exercise might yield more than one potential venture. Then ask yourself another critical question, "How do I prioritize these opportunities?" How will you decide which one offers the highest impact down to the least impact?

The Business Consultant

Often, it may be that you need to seek out advice to determine what course of action is needed. A good business consultant can be invaluable in this situation, especially if you have a specialized skill and the desire to start a business but don't have the experience of starting one.

Let me give you an example. I have good friends, Reggie and Ladye Smith, who live in Nashville, TN, and who record and perform in the Christian music business. Several years ago, they were at a crossroads in determining their next move from a business standpoint. They had several opportunities to produce different CDs. They also had multiple opportunities to promote their music, some under another company's promotion as well as an option to self-promote. Not only are they married with a child, but are also business partners. This makes it hard to have business conversations decoupled from the everyday decisions of family life. So, I offered to help them strategically plan for the next chapter in their careers.

Since I had some knowledge of the music business, I had an idea of the business decisions that needed to be made. I also had experience in strategically planning and assisting people and companies to think differently about their choices. After a one-day planning session, they made a series of decisions about issues that had previously crippled their business (spilling over to their marriage) and completely changed their focus of business activity. They faithfully executed the plan we outlined that day.

As I check in with them from time to time, not only is their business stronger than ever, but they also have a process to make decisions decoupled from their family life. Reaching out to an external resource may be needed to solidify the strategic direction you need to take. Don't hesitate to invest in a quality consultant you have interviewed and you feel can assist you in making good decisions.

Try It. You May Like It.

I would like to specifically talk for a moment to younger readers, perhaps those early in their career, budding entrepreneurs and future leaders. If you are outside of this group, feel free to skip ahead to Chapter 9.

So, ask yourself these questions: What is it I want to do? What's my strategic direction? Perhaps you've heard of the story of a young man sitting on the beach, watching the ships coming in and out of the port, waiting for his ship to come in. When his ship comes, he will know it. He will get on that ship and become part of that crew.

Well, I don't agree with that. There are some problems with that scenario, the biggest of which is sitting on the beach won't tell you anything about where that ship has been, about the quality of the captain, about the rest of the crew, or what their particular strategic direction is. The man on the beach has no idea what he likes and dislikes. He's just sitting on the beach, waiting.

When I get a chance to speak with young people about career options, I always encourage action. To whatever extent you are able, as soon as you can, get a job. Try working different jobs. Work in retail. Work in the service industry. Work in food service. Work a bunch of different jobs. Through those experiences, you will get some ideas about what your skills are.

Are you a people person or are you more of a lone wolf? Are you a service-oriented person or are you more of a craftsman? Do you work better with your hands or with your head? These skills could apply to literally thousands of different jobs. You will know your strengths and weaknesses only when you've actually gone out and done some things that give you a frame of reference for whether you're good at something or not.

Even at the early age of thirteen, I was working at a small, local grocery store near my home. Because I looked a lot older than I was, people assumed I was an adult, so I took an air of authority and started acting like an assistant manager. Everyone I encountered believed I was a manager, even though I was only thirteen years old! Before that, I had a paper route. I mowed lawns. At sixteen, I went to work for my brother at his gas station. In college, I worked construction and as a waiter at an oyster bar, shucking oysters and chatting up customers, earning tips. These are the types of jobs that I highly encourage young people to do as early as possible, so they can start to understand their skills.

Follow a Good Captain

Now, go back to the story of the young man sitting on the beach, but now it's you, waiting for your ship to come. You have no idea what you're good at, what you might like, or what you might not like. You may not hear this often, but what you really need to do is look at the captain (boss, manager, etc.) of each ship. Find somebody exhibiting good leadership who you think would make a good captain, who takes care of his crew no matter what, and then it won't matter where that captain's going. You get on that ship and you follow that captain throughout that particular journey, whatever that is. You spend six months, arrive at the destination, performing various jobs along the way, and find out that you hate it! You don't want anything to do with that job, but you selected a good captain, and he took care of his crew. Now you know something that you don't like, but you learned a lot from that captain.

Take that knowledge with you on the next journey. You now know a career you don't want to do for the rest of your life, so you abandon that ship at the next port, find another good captain, hop on board another ship, and go another direction. I believe that only through action, only through experiencing career options, will you complete the process of selecting your personal strategic direction. Even reading and studying cannot replace personal experience to know what you like and dislike, what you're good at and what you're not good at.

As an individual and ultimately as a manager and business owner, I always try to be direct and honest with myself about what I'm good at and what I'm not. I focus my time and attention on the things I'm good at, and then hire people who have the skills in my weak areas. I rely on them to augment those weaknesses, so we can have more success in the company.

Let me clearly say to younger readers that any job you have in a company is not about you. It's about your employer. There is a particular job to be done, they have created a job description, and have hired you to do that job. Pour yourself into that job and excel to every extent possible. But if that job doesn't pan out for you, if you are uninspired by the work, it is not the employer's responsibility to create job requirements around your personal interests. Seek out employers whose goals align with yours and then become a star for that company. Or start your own company. But don't spend any time in an attitude of entitlement about what your employer should be doing for you.

"You Only Worked There for Three Months?"

To think you're going to sit around and wait and somehow this magical career or job will come to you is unwise. It just doesn't work that way. You need to climb aboard and get a job. A lot of people are frightened to stay at a job only three to six months and then move on, concerned that it will look bad on their resume.

Potential employers will see a short tenure posting on your resume, and ask, "Well, why were you only at this company for three months?"

You answer, "I took that job because I wanted training in a certain skill," or "I was looking for a certain type of experience, and I found out that is not what I wanted to do, so I moved on to something else."

Now, as someone who has hired a lot of people, I would greatly respect hearing somebody say, "I tried several jobs and learned what I liked and did not like, what I was good at and what I was not good at." I'm much more concerned about big gaps in time in their employment sequence.

Somebody might say, "Well, I was looking for another job."

You couldn't find any job anywhere?

"Well, no. I was looking for a certain type of position."

Now, some gaps in a resume do happen and you don't need to be embarrassed about them. But I personally applaud somebody who flips burgers or does anything productive while they're in the process of looking for the job they want because that shows initiative. They're showing they're willing to be doing something, perhaps even something outside of what they might normally do just to know if that job was something that a) they might be good at or b) they might like or be interested in.

Now, in all things, moderation. If I see that a potential employee is frequently jumping from one company to the next and has no good explanation other than they thought working for six companies in a year and a half was a means of advancement, then I might be wary of that employee. It takes time to know for sure if this new job is a good fit; if a person jumps ship at the earliest point of unease, it could signal a lack of perseverance. Plus, remember that it's expensive and counterproductive for your employer to hire a new employee only to have them leave right at the moment that they should start being useful. Once you are into your professional years, your resume and job history will follow you everywhere, so plan carefully for what story it will tell.

CHAPTER NINE
Making the Best of a Bad Situation

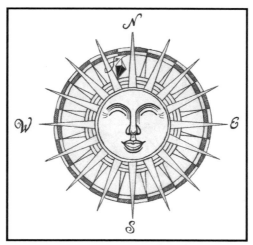

*"Man is fully responsible for his nature
and his choices."*

— Jean-Paul Sartre

*We turned the boat around and set a new course ... again! This time
we were headed in a southwesterly direction. The whole chain of
events since waking up that morning to find the Bahamas missing
unnerved all of us. We were already tired from lack of sleep on the
passage over and the steady anxiety over what in the world could be
happening.*

This area of the Atlantic falls within the Bermuda Triangle, a triangular area of roughly a million square miles, in which many ships and planes have been reported lost or encountered strange occurrences with navigation equipment. In my mind, it was possible we might be another victim of this weird phenomenon. Something was surely wonky with our compass. What if it was still not working properly? How would we know we were not still moving in the wrong direction? We stayed alert all through the day, looking for any signs of land, even though we should have been napping and restoring our minds and bodies. Vince was anxious, and I'm sure he had doubts that my dad and I knew what we were doing.

By the time we saw what turned out to be, indeed, West End, night had fallen upon us. There was the bright white light shining at the tip of the harbor! Our relief was great, yet we were arriving at the treacherous opening of the channel in the dark of a nearly moonless night. We considered two options: find an anchorage or drift in deep water until daylight came again.

The area around this part of the Bahamas is full of small cays and spits of land, lined with jagged coral reefs just under the surface on the Atlantic side and shallow sand bars on the inner side. Not too far out from the edge of the entire Grand Bahamas Bank, the ocean is deep, far too deep for our anchor line. Going into the channel in the absolute darkness would almost certainly mean running aground. Therefore, we determined that anchoring the Alacrity for the night was not an option. We motored several miles away and prepared her to drift in deep water by putting out the sea anchor, a large canvas bag on a line that looks like a windsock. This device would keep the bow in line with the current and wind and slow her drift.

I was elated we had received new information putting us back on course, but I was also concerned we may still not be on the right path. After all, what made the guys on the other boat experts? What if they were wrong? Due to how mentally and physically tired we were, I think we were ready to believe anyone who told us about how to get back on course. Certainly we were not in a position to verify what they were telling us. In the absence of any other viable information to the contrary, whatever is the most likely course must be the one you follow.

Fortunately for us, their advice was accurate. We were, in fact, going in the right direction, and we did reach the outskirts of West End, Bahamas, that day. We could see the lights of the town! When you talk about the light at the end of a tunnel or other kind of metaphor about seeing a light in the darkness, it certainly applied to us in that moment. We were elated to see those lights!

Think about it. Since we left Florida around ten o'clock the previous night, we had not seen anything but blackness by night and the open vast ocean by day. So, to come in and see all those lights and to know we had arrived at the correct destination was an amazing feeling.

But, now we were faced with a choice. The *Alacrity* drew nearly five feet from the waterline down to her keel. So, we had to be extremely careful about where we went, so as not to hit the coral, particularly on the open-water side of the small island cays between the Bahamas and the United States. The water on that side gets quite deep, quite fast. Then, there's the inner part, within the Grand Bahamas Bank. There are spans of open water, but a lot of it is shallow with a sandy bottom, in many cases less than three feet deep. If the bottom of the boat touched that sandy part, it wouldn't damage the hull, but the boat could easily run aground. Then, depending on the tides, you could be stuck there for hours. To run aground is no small matter and was always an immediate concern when sailing the Bahamas.

Our Choices

We had three choices. We could go ahead, take our chances, slowly find the channel, and get inside the inlet where we could find an anchorage in the safe harbor. Once inside, we could have even gone to the local marina and docked. We never docked there because it cost money, and you can anchor for free. It certainly would have been a relief to safely be at dock and get a good night's sleep. But, unlike the United States, which has not only green and red colored markers indicating the channels by day but also has many of those markers lighted at night, the Bahamas did not offer that luxury. We would have gone into the harbor blind.

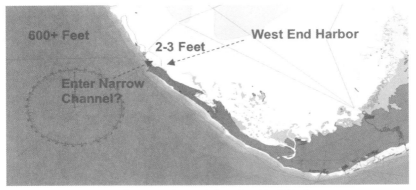

Map showing channel for West End Harbor
and the relative depth of the water

As tempting as it was to just go in there and be safe, it was incredibly risky. We would have likely grounded the boat. Another option was to find a place shallow enough to anchor. Again, this was all before GPS and electronic charts. At the time, a lot of the little islands and cays were not even on the paper charts. They're small sand outcroppings, basically coral formations that form an island that may only be a couple hundred square feet in size. They're scattered all over the Grand Bahamas Bank. To try and find a safe place to anchor wasn't that great a prospect anyway. Right next to the islands, it is prohibitively shallow and full of sharp coral but, even a hundred feet offshore, the water could easily be hundreds of feet deep.

Because of the depth of the water, we could not anchor offshore; our anchor line was too short. The rule of thumb is to have five to seven feet of anchor line for every foot of the depth of the water. So, if the water is one hundred feet deep, you should have six hundred feet of anchor line. We didn't have anywhere close to that amount: our anchor chain and line together was probably about 250 feet. Even if our anchor could reach bottom, it would end up at too steep of an angle relative to the anchor, which would just drag along the bottom. We might have had the impression we were secure since our anchor was out, but, in actuality, we would have been drifting.

Ignoring Valid Options

Also understand we were just weary, bone-tired, stressed, and sleep-deprived. We were not thinking clearly, yet we were still hyper-focused, trying hard to make good decisions while knowing we were predisposed to not thinking clearly.

What my dad ultimately decided to do was put out the sea anchor. This anchor looks like a big windsock you might see at a small, regional airport. It's big and heavy, made of canvas. He tied it to a cleat at the bow of the *Alacrity*, and it kept her facing relatively into the wind and current instead of wildly swinging from one side to the other. It essentially kept us in a stable orientation, still drifting but not going wildly off course.

The sea anchor was the only viable option we had. Well, that is not exactly true. We could have braved the open channel in the dark and attempted to safely anchor inside of the Grand Bahamas Bank. We didn't consider this option because a) we knew there was a large probability we would run aground and b) we never considered the possibility that we might drift onto a coral cay, smashing a hole in the boat.

In hindsight, had we carefully examined both of these as realistic possibilities, we would have headed into the channel because running aground on the sandy bottom of the inner Bahamas Bank is an infinitely better option than running aground on coral.

Nearly forty years later, it's easy to see that potentially grounding the boat was a better option than putting out the sea anchor and setting up a watch. This is an example of counterfactual thinking. Counterfactual thinking is a concept in psychology involving the human tendency to create possible alternatives to life events that have already occurred, something that is contrary to what actually happened.

Counterfactual thinking is exactly as it states: "counter to the facts." These thoughts consist of "What if?" and "If I had only..." statements that occur when thinking of how things could have turned out differently. Counterfactual thoughts focus on circumstances that could never possibly happen in real-time because they pertain to events that occurred in the past. Hindsight is not only 20/20, but it has the benefit of a great night's sleep. At the time, wrecking the boat on a cay wasn't an option we considered. But we should have. The reasons for considering this possibility include:

• Knowing of the existence of many small cays and knowing they had coral formations on the ocean side.

• Knowing that running aground inside the Bahamas Bank was not fatal. In fact, we had run aground inside the Grand Bahamas Bank before with no disastrous effect.

• Knowing that we were exhausted and the probability of falling asleep was high.

So, why didn't we weigh the risk of grounding the boat on a coral cay versus the risk of grounding the boat on the sandy inner bank? Grounding the boat was a Black Swan event, an "unthinkable" event, that didn't enter our minds. By not considering this possibility, we gave ourselves an incomplete list of choices from which to choose.

The critical question we left out of our decision was this, "What is the worst that can happen?" Asking that question would have yielded the following:

• If we go into the channel, we could run aground on the sandy bottom and be stuck until the tide changed.

- If we stay outside and use the sea anchor, we could drift into a cay and smash the bottom of the boat on the sharp coral.

Faced with these two scenarios, it seems obvious which one represents the less "risky" course of action. Yet, as we saw it at the time, our choices were:

- If we go into the channel, we could run aground on the sandy bottom and be stuck until the tide changed.

- If we stay outside and use the sea anchor, we could drift away from the channel and once daylight arrived, we would safely motor into the inner Bahamas Bank.

Do you see that by not looking at all the choices facing you from a realistic "what could really happen" perspective, you will be making a choice from a list of options that may be dangerously incomplete?

We tend to downplay the negative aspects of potential decisions with statements like "That would never happen," or "The chances of that happening are nil." However, if you focus on what could reasonably occur and then make sure all of the options are considered from the most reasonable negative impact, then you should be able to make a rational choice from a complete and accurate list of options.

Reasonable Choices

Note that I am talking about reasonable potential outcomes. In the case of the *Alacrity*, running aground on cays that we knew to exist, cays that would be nearly impossible to see in the dark, was a reasonable potential outcome. We might have also considered that a giant squid could have come up from the depths to drag our boat down like a Kraken spiced black rum commercial. Or a meteor could have struck the ship. Neither of those is particularly reasonable. At least they are significantly less likely than running aground in the dark. There is no need to get really crazy with options that are not reasonable.

Consider what reasonable options you are leaving out of your matrix of choices. When you are facing a crisis, your ability to make good decisions is challenged. You may not be sleep-deprived, but your adrenaline may be up. Critical decisions need to be made, and the pressure is on. Lots of people are looking to you for answers and guidance. If you are not including all of the relevant information regarding the choices you have, then you are leaving open the possibility you will not arrive at a desirable positive outcome. The question then becomes, "How can I have a reasonable assurance I am including all rational options?" Let's examine some ways.

Options When Time Is Not a Factor

First, we must address the issue of time. Do you have time to thoughtfully weigh out matters? As we discussed in Chapter 3, there are situations where you don't have time to sit and think for an hour about what your options are.

So, setting aside the emergency situation where you have to quickly choose an option, let's assume you have time to think. How will you accumulate all of the reasonable options for a response to the crisis? Here are some thoughts for your consideration:

- Make a list of all obvious options – I would explain more about this here, but that would negate the fact that I said these would be obvious. Well, maybe it isn't that obvious to everyone. What I mean is start first with the options you absolutely know are possibilities. Capture all of those as quickly as possible.

- Brainstorm – Gather a group of trusted individuals and brainstorm the question, "What are all the options we can consider for situation X?" You should carefully consider who would be in this brainstorming group. Including individuals from different levels and areas of the organization will give you a better chance of coming up with unique options. If you have four key managers and they all think similarly to you, perhaps have worked together with you for many years, then how different will the options they brainstorm be? Adding in people with diverse skills can move you to think "outside the box." Include at least one true contrarian. Sometimes, even though people are throwing out "bad" ideas, or shooting down potentially good ones, they will spark you to think of an option you may not have otherwise considered.

- Reverse Brainstorm – If you get stuck on brainstorming options but feel you have not tapped into all of the possibilities you should be considering, then try a reverse brainstorm. By reversing the premise of the brainstorming question, you can often unlock other possibilities. Here's an example of a reverse brainstorm. Say you want to increase the number of people that take public transportation. Regular brainstorming would yield ways to encourage more bus and subway riders. The reverse would be to brainstorm all of the ways you could discourage people from using public transportation. This usually gets some items on the page quickly. Once you have a new list of potential ways you can discourage use of the buses and subway, examine each of those individually to determine what the opposite of that element is. For example, if reverse brainstorming yielded an idea to make the buses and subways dark and filthy, the reverse would be having them clean and brightly lit. This reverse brainstorming should yield options that may not have been included in the original brainstorming list.

- Tap into outside resources – By having a list of consultants, friends whose advice you trust, or a network of potential advisors (such as LinkedIn), you can provide a scenario and ask for potential options for resolution. A larger group raises the likelihood you will get a good option or two to add to your decision matrix.

Decision Time

At some point, you have to make a decision. Determine in advance how much time you have to gather options. Set a deadline. When that time arrives, unless you have a strong chance of discovering additional reasonable options, put all of the options on a chart and decide a) the likelihood each option will lead to a positive result and b) the worst that could occur by taking each option.

If you have time, you can even create a simple three-column spreadsheet that shows each option, its potential for success, and wort-case scenario. Usually, when you can look at all the options and see both the positive and negative ramifications, the appropriate course of action becomes clearer. In the case of the *Alacrity*, that spreadsheet might have looked like this:

Option	Best Possible Outcome	Worst Possible Outcome
Head into Bahamas Bank via harbor channel	– Out of danger – Able to find safe anchorage – Everybody can go to sleep	Strong possibility of running aground, since there is no visibility and could be stuck on sandy bottom for undetermined amount of time
Anchor in open water (requiring us to be relatively close to shore)	–Anchor holds and we remain in one place until morning –Everybody can go to sleep	Almost certainly, our anchor line would not have been long enough to allow anchor to hold and boat would drift away, potentially crashing into coral cay
Use sea anchor in open water (this would mean going further away from shore but still within sight of harbor lights)	–Sea anchor keeps us in relative position and we remain safely offshore until morning –Requires someone to be awake	Sea anchor does not hold us in relative position and, due to darkness, there is no way to know where the boat is drifting, potentially crashing into coral cay

Option	Best Possible Outcome	Worst Possible Outcome
GIANT SQUID ATTACK! *(Sorry, I couldn't help myself.)*	WE FIGHT THE SQUID LIKE 20,000 LEAGUES UNDER THE SEA AND HAVE THE LARGEST CALAMARI STEAK ON RECORD.	WE ARE DRAGGED DOWN TO THE DEPTHS AND ARE MEMORIALIZED ON A BLACK SPICED RUM COMMERCIAL.

What are the two things that stand out when you look at the table of options above? Forget the craziness of the giant squid attack. Under the worst scenario, grounding the boat on sand inside the Bahamas Bank seems pretty tame compared to wrecking the boat on coral, which was possible with the other two options.

Under the best possible scenario, two of the options allowed for the crew to sleep, one required someone to stay awake. So, if chancing the channel was the best of the worst options and was also one of the two choices that allowed the crew to sleep, it seems reasonable that we should have chosen that option. Ah, gotta love that hindsight thinkin'!

We chose to deploy the sea anchor and wait until morning. We maneuvered out a little further on the deep-water side, a safe distance away from the shoreline, maybe a couple of miles. The thinking was that we were far enough away that, even if we drifted some back to shore, it would not be enough to put us in danger.

We put the sea anchor out and made a plan for my dad and me to trade off keeping watch. We did not ask Vince to take a watch since he was so inexperienced and already frazzled. Tomorrow, we would be safely anchored inside the Bahamas Bank and all of the day's struggles would be just a grand story to tell.

CHAPTER TEN
The Outfitting

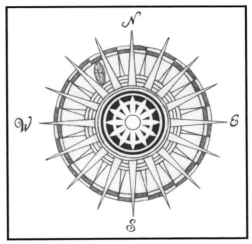

*"Only someone who is well prepared
has the opportunity to improvise."*

— Ingmar Bergman

To this point in the book, I've noted specific comparisons of the *Grafton* and the *Invercauld* and their respective captains. The journals that Musgrave and Raynal kept give specific details about how they prepared for their journey. As you consider starting a new company or maybe a big expansion of your business, embarking on a new career after graduation from college, or changing careers, perhaps you have an attitude of careful preparation.

All these goals have equivalent preparations, similar to how a ship's captain might work toward getting ready for a journey. Don't make the same mistake Musgrave made—traveling well down the path toward your goal and then starting to skimp on critical elements.

Provisions

As a part of the whole outfitting of the *Grafton*, Uncle Musgrave and Sarpy budgeted a certain amount of money. With that budget, Captain Musgrave and Raynal did a couple of very important things, one of which was to change the configuration of the ship in order to handle the type of sailing required and to hold the ore they wished to bring back from their original destination, Campbell Island. They also put in ten tons of sandstone blocks as ballast in the bottom of the hull because they wanted it to sit more securely in the water.

Having completed the changes to the *Grafton*, they continued the pre-trip process by acquiring all of the provisions. They planned for a four-month expedition, a preliminary prospecting trip. They weren't planning to come back with tons of ore; they would go to the island, find this hoped-for mother lode of argentiferous tin, mine enough to come back and certify that, yes, it was silver-bearing, stake a claim, and then return with larger vessels and mine it.

They bought twenty casks of fresh water, three hundred pounds of ship's bread (large crackers made out of water and flour baked so hard you could break a tooth biting one), two barrels of salt pork, twenty gallons of molasses, a barrel of salt beef, two hundred pounds of ordinary flour, some cartons of sugar and butter, a bag of dried beans, a bag of peas, ten pounds of coffee, ten pounds of tea, and a couple of barrels of potatoes, as well as spare canvas, rope, and spars. With this task done, they had nearly completed provisioning the boat. Now came a critical point. The money from Uncle Musgrave and Sarpy ran out.

Ninety Feet of Anchor Line

However, Musgrave hadn't purchased chain for the *Grafton's* anchors yet. He had two anchors, both vital for a number of reasons. If you lose one, you have another, so there's a backup. Also, in many cases, if you only have one anchor out, the boat can move in a big arc. In fact, it could move all the way around in a full circle, depending on winds and currents. In order to avoid that, especially if drifting in a big arc might take you into danger, you put an anchor out in the front of the boat, let out a significant amount of anchor line, and then set an anchor in the back. You pull the anchor line in the front back in, so the boat is in the middle of two anchors that might be 150 feet apart. The two anchors, bow and stern, will hold the boat in a relatively stable position. Musgrave ran out of money, and he hadn't yet purchased this critical provision: anchor chain.

Remember, you need seven times the amount of anchor line as the depth of the water. If the depth of the water is ten feet, you need seventy feet of anchor line out. If you're using all chain, you can maybe knock that down to five times the amount of line, so if you were anchoring in a hundred feet of water, you would need five hundred feet of chain.

Captain Musgrave insisted on acquiring more capital for the chain and line needed, but Uncle Musgrave and Sarpy refused to provide any additional funds. After much back and forth bickering, they agreed to provide some additional money, but not enough to buy the quality of chain they needed or the length required. They wound up with 180 feet of low-grade chain, and that had to serve both anchors!

Consider this situation: Musgrave has outfitted his ship. He's bought all these provisions. He's made all these changes to the ship to weather the trip. Now, he's about to set off with only ninety feet of chain for each of those anchors. Ninety feet of chain! Even if you go with the most aggressive estimate, five times the depth of the water as opposed to seven times, that ninety feet of line would allow him to anchor in no more than eighteen feet of water. If they were in a sheltered area, close to the shore, it's possible they could anchor in less than eighteen feet of water, but for them to go on this extended expedition with that small amount of chain was just … foolish.

As an experienced seaman, he should have said, "Look! If we don't have the right quality and proper amount of chain for these an-chors, we can't undertake the mission," and stopped the voyage right there.

This happens all the time in business. You have a budget for some new expansion or new project, but you've underestimated the cost or perhaps you have cost overruns. You may say, "Well, I've invested so much. Look at all the money and time we've spent to start this venture, and now we're short of funds to get what we need. We've got to go ahead and complete it. Do whatever it takes to finish."

You wind up skimping, spending very little on some incredibly important, key elements. One of the lessons here is to start with the most important items and spend down to the least important items.

If you have to outfit a ship, you look at all the different items and ask, "What will be the most important to us? What will we really need if we have a crisis? What are the tools we must have?"

If Captain Musgrave had applied this principle, he would have put quality anchor chain in sufficient lengths near the top of the provision list, and he would have purchased that first. After that, he would know what else they could afford. If he had thought through everything needed for the trip and set a budget to acquire those things, then clearly the quality and amount of chain was not properly accounted for in that budget. He should have started from the very beginning with an understanding of what the expedition was going to require.

What would be the cost for all the necessary components of the right quality before ever setting out? I think the strategic error here is taking something as important as the anchor chain and leaving it for last, then having to skimp on it both in quality and in amount. That substandard chain is directly linked to why they couldn't hold the ship's position when they ultimately wrecked on Auckland Island.

Properly Outfitted

Assuming you do have a strategic direction and are confident about what you're doing (you may even have a Plan B or a Plan C in mind), you can now focus on the critically important infrastructure to achieve that strategic direction. Consider the classic four-box grid showing whether or not you have a good plan and good infrastructure—having the right equipment, the right tools—to achieve your objectives.

	Bad Infrastructure	Good Infrastructure
Good Plan	Potential problems. Like the *Grafton*, even though you might be working your plan A or B effectively, the lack of proper infra-structure leaves you at risk of failure.	Optimal situation. You have planned well, and you have all of the required elements of sufficient quality to rea-sonably make the venture a success.
Bad Plan	Likely disaster. Having no plan leaves you adrift, with no specific purpose. You have no idea what might come your way, so you don't have any particular infrastructure to mitigate a serious problem.	Things could still work out. Even though your plan is bad, you can still pivot and act on new opportunities and effectively use the quality infrastructure you have to reach success.

I'm not saying you have to create the perfect environment to be successful. Obviously, there are some companies, organizations, and individuals who grind it out and persevere without having all of the resources they need, and still become successful. But it's much, much harder, right? So, only in a situation where you have established a good strategic direction and properly outfitted your organization with the appropriate resources needed to achieve that direction will you see optimal success.

Latest and Greatest

Start with the elements you already know. In the field of software development, even though you might be writing a program to do something that's never been done before, the elements you need to be successful are well-known. You need smart people who understand the programming language you're working with. You need tools for the actual programming software, like the database and all the individual elements required software-wise in order for you to compile the finished code. You need business analysts who understand the particular business problem you're trying to solve. You need documentation writers. You need quality assurance technicians.

You already know you need the elements to create a proper software product. But within that known set of required elements, there's still a constant struggle to know whether or not you're using the most recent technology. In my experience, technical people always want to use the latest and greatest tools! As an executive in the process, you must negotiate the balance between whether the resources you have are adequate and whether you have to buy the newest versions of programming tools. In my opinion, you don't have to constantly stay on the bleeding edge of technology, but you certainly cannot be so far behind in terms of the tools you're using that your people are working inefficiently and becoming frustrated.

Know What You're Looking For

Think about this in the context of the two ship captains. We don't know very much about how the *Invercauld* was chosen or whether Dalgarno had any say in choosing it. Perhaps he was told, "Take this ship and go to South America and pick up fertilizer." But we do know a good bit from their diaries about how Musgrave and Raynal selected the *Grafton*. They were looking for particular components in a ship related to what they planned to do. They passed up numerous ships because they had a definite idea about what they needed, and they would only buy a ship that met the requirements for their strategic direction—they were going to hunt for this ore. That was their strategic direction. At the same time, they knew they were going to have a small crew, so it had to be a ship that could be handled by the limited number of sailors they were planning to take.

They considered all these factors before ultimately choosing the *Grafton*. From Joan Druett's book, you get the idea that when they saw the ship it had sort of a shimmering glow, and they heard this angelic choir. (The image I conjure up in my mind is the classic scene from *Wayne's World* when Wayne goes to the music store to look at the electric guitar he covets. "It will be mine. Oh yes, it will be mine.")[6] They had looked at so many different ships, but it was obvious to them this was the one; it met all of the requirements. They bought it, even though it cost more than they had planned to spend.

Hmmm, maybe this threw the budget off, so they couldn't afford the proper chain! When you are working your budget, you could be more aggressive with expense projections to account for this very type of situation. Make sure you have the budget to purchase everything you need!

Expensive but Necessary

In the software development business, one of the most important, though relatively unsung, tasks is quality assurance or QA. QA is all about testing the software to make sure what you program actually works correctly as designed. Not only do you need to test new functionality, but (perhaps more importantly) you need to make sure in building something new that you haven't broken existing code. As you're developing software and adding features, are you creating bugs that weren't even a target of whatever you were trying to upgrade?

---

6 If you are not familiar with *Wayne's World*, here is the scene I am referring to: https://www.youtube.com/watch?v=a7jJnwEeiU0. Watch the whole movie. It's a hoot!

Quality assurance can be quite a laborious, manual process, requiring somebody to walk through a script of dozens or even hundreds of different tasks, interacting with the software directly, inputting different data fields that are expected to get a specific result, as well as entering in data fields that should generate an error message. QA has this grind-it-out aspect—executing hundreds of permutations in order to understand whether or not the software is producing the desired result.

The people who do this work do not always find it particularly joyful or fulfilling. It's boring a lot of the time. So, they want access to an automated tool that runs through those tasks. A tool like this removes the need for the mind-numbing, rote aspects of the job, freeing the QA person to focus on the creation of scripts and the discovery of ways they can break the system, ensuring that it's functioning properly. They will not spend hours just plucking away at the keyboard.

We now have software to automatically run scripts. It's a ginormous pain to create all these scripts individually. You have to program the system to do a series of tasks as if you were actually doing them. It's quite time-consuming and meticulous to set that up. But once it's up, you run the program overnight, and it will crank out hundreds or thousands or tens of thousands of permutations of data. When you return, you only have to look at those places where the software did not perform as expected. This allows the QA technician to focus on the exceptions and create bug reports, so the development team can fix the bugs.

As you can imagine, this type of software is pricey. This is a great example of what I'm talking about. Is it possible for a software manufacturer to test software and not have one of these automated tools? Sure. Absolutely possible. However, depending on the breadth and scope of the software you're developing, it may become necessary, a requirement, for you to have these automated tools. If you don't make that investment, most likely, you're not going to keep the interest of the people doing that job. They're going to get sick of it and decide to work at a company that does have automated testing tools. Also, you're most likely not going to finish testing all the different permutations you need to in order to assure the software is operating properly within the time constraints most projects operate. Either of those scenarios will have a negative impact on your goal of successfully launching a software product.

Ask yourself: do I have all the tools I need to achieve my objective? Consider this question in terms of operational and programming issues, but also marketing, sales, accounting, HR, and financing. All elements and areas of the company need to be examined to see if your employees have the right tools to do their jobs well. You should be able to sit down and say, "If we're going to fulfill our strategic plan, if we're going to be successful, here's what we need in order to achieve that. Here's what our people need to be successful and happy about their jobs. Here's what will accelerate our processes past manual effort."

I remember doing this a few years ago with a company for which I was performing strategic planning. As a part of that, we incorporated into their vision how many additional people would have to be hired in order for them to achieve success, so HR knew the head count was likely going to increase in the next year. Therefore, when they created their budgets, they included people they needed—not only the cost of finding those people but also the cost of hiring them, bringing them in, training them, managing them, and insuring them.

This is the attitude to have: I'm not just looking at strategic planning from a technical standpoint,but holistically throughout the entire company related to resources. What do I need to have in order for my plan to succeed? Do I have the appropriate funding for all of that?

Remove Obstacles

Senior managers and business owners, removing obstacles is priority number three. (Quick reminder: 1. Hire the right people. 2. Create and communicate a strategic direction.) When I think about all the different senior management positions I've held, particularly the opportunities to be CEO, I start thinking about what my job ultimately entailed. While hiring people and determining strategic direction are more important, they are not always an ongoing activity.

A constant activity is removing obstacles, removing any barriers that might prevent your team's success. That might mean acquiring additional software or tools. That might mean changing work schedules to accommodate when team members are at their peak efficiency. It could mean looking at ways to find alternative channels for you to deliver or distribute your software, to find other means and mechanisms by which you can get software into the hands of more customers. Continue this process of asking, "What would keep us from success? Where are the barriers to success? How can I eliminate those barriers?"

It is highly unlikely that you have unlimited funding.[7] Take a look at your budget and ask, "What's the best possible use of that capital to remove barriers and give me the greatest possible chance of success?" Perhaps you brainstorm a list of activities that would be classified as removing barriers. You might be able to look at the list and easily sort them in order. But, in some cases, that might be difficult.

---

7 Wait. I'm positive you don't have unlimited funding. Wait again. If you do have unlimited funding, I want you to contact me, today, so we can start a business together because I've got lots of ideas. Here's my email address: david@davidpeterson.com.

So, here are a few suggestions:

1. Gather more information. The reason you may not be able to immediately tell where something fits in the order of priority may simply be you don't have enough information about how much of a barrier it is. Find additional data to understand the relative size of the barrier you're going to be able to remove. I know of a business owner who was trying to address the stress, long hours, and tight project deadlines in the office. He brought in a couple of massage technicians and encouraged employees to sign up for massages every week. Now, that was way cool. I happened to be at their office on massage day, and I got one. It definitely reduced the stress in the office and made people feel better about the difficulties associated with a long and grueling project. But would that be more beneficial than knowing that there was a particular bug in the database system you were using or that Microsoft had issued a bulletin indicating that there was an issue in the current version of the operating system that could be the cause of your issue?

2. Determine how many employees are affected. If there is something you can do that will affect a significant number of employees, all other things being equal, it should have a higher priority than something that affects only a few or one. Having said that, it all goes back to your available funds. If you can afford to do five or six small things for different groups of employees, that may have a greater impact than one thing that affects every employee but is very costly.

3. Is it something "hard," related to executing the basic business activity or "soft," related to people and their attitude toward their job? Depending on the type of business you are in, something hard, like periodic maintenance on a key piece of equipment, may be more important to the success of the business versus offering weekly massages. The more people-

oriented your business is, the more important it is to provide obstacle-removing elements that change how people feel about their jobs. The emotional connection between a person's job and relative happiness is a big deal.

Small Changes Can Make a Big Impact

You have to prioritize. If you have multiple barrier-breaking items on the list related to software development, such as automated quality assurance testing tools, updated database tools, and massages for the team, I wouldn't automatically assume that massages would be last, but you must look at the relative impact of each item.

You might assume that massages would have a much greater effect across a wider range of employees. Not necessarily so. Let's say, out of twenty support technicians, twelve of them would really enjoy the massages and eight of them wouldn't want anyone to put their hands on them for any reason whatsoever. But all twenty of them would greatly appreciate an updated help desk tool. You need a mechanism, a methodology, for deciding how to allocate money for updating tools or removing roadblocks, for making people's jobs easier or more effective. I've provided a blueprint for creating a decision methodology at the end of this chapter. Some relatively small things can have a big impact.

For example, technical people especially value large monitors and multiple monitors, so they don't have to switch back and forth between different programs on one screen. It's a constant issue— high-end technical staff fighting and fussing over monitors. You know what? These monitors are now so inexpensive. Go out and buy more. Let every one of those little cubicles look like a NASA command center trying to bring Apollo 13 back home. Fine. You want monitors? You got 'em. Stack them up. Whatever you want to do.

I don't want anybody grousing or fussing that they don't have multiple monitors. Does having more monitors increase employee efficiency? While there is some reduction in switching back and forth between programs, the amount of actual time savings is minimally important. But, I see this issue repeated at every single company I work with, particularly with technical people. Just buy the monitors, and don't spend much time trying to understand why they're super important because, at the end of the day, they're not that expensive. If the technical staff "feels" more comfortable with dual monitors and they feel better about their company and their job, they will work harder, maybe even smarter. Also consider the decor. It may sound silly, but designing a creative workspace is critical for helping people to think and work creatively. Even if you are not in a creative field, having space, or at least part of the space, where employees can enjoy each other and have fun is an important element.

Continuing Education

What keeps people excited about coming to work? In addition to using the latest tools, they want to have opportunities to increase their skill set. Consider the value of education and the need to properly budget for it as a part of reaching your strategic destination. More and more of the jobs out there are less and less about manual labor. We have more service industry, technical, and professional jobs. People expect a scientist, a computer programmer, a nurse, or a doctor to constantly upgrade their education.

But what if you're a welder or an automobile mechanic? Those fields are incredibly important. In fact, automobile mechanic may become one of the higher paying jobs as it gets more and more advanced. My point is that certain careers that formerly did not require significant ongoing education do, in fact, require continuing education to remain qualified. These days, an automobile mechanic who attains a certain level of knowledge but never increases that knowledge will find, within just a few years, that his knowledge is out of date and will no longer work on newer model cars. Certainly, computer programming and numerous other technical fields are the same way.

With that in mind, consider how critically important it is to offer education opportunities to your staff. By making continuing education an element of the approved budget, allocating the time needed to obtain new knowledge, and adding requirements for tailored ongoing education will ensure that your employees know how important continuing education is to you.

Ongoing education is a critical element you can integrate into everybody's job description and annual review. You can require ongoing education at different levels from your people, and you're going to fund it. You're going to fund whatever educational opportunities are necessary by including that education in the budget.

Let's go back to creating software. Think about people with specialized computer skills. They really don't ask for a lot. They want to be able to dress casually. They certainly don't want to have to dress up. They want multiple monitors. They want to have a reasonably hip workspace and access to places where they can blow off some steam and let their right brain think. But what they value even more than a hip workspace or even salary in some cases is the ability to extend their education—to get additional certifications, to go to an advanced Microsoft school or earn database certifications, and to get additional types of training on the new development tools when they are released. They want to be able to extend their education and their contacts. They want to find like-minded people with whom they can communicate.

If they encounter a vexing problem at work, and they're struggling to figure out what that is, they can call somebody they met at a conference or training and say, "Hey, I'm struggling with this.

Have you encountered this?"

"Oh, yeah. Let me show you what I've figured out."

That kind of networking is critically important to many employees in terms of how positively they feel about their job.

Invest in Your People

From a business owner's standpoint, if employee satisfaction and knowledge were the only reasons to offer more education, they would be reasons enough. Now, think about a manufacturer that has large-scale equipment used to make a particular product. Think about the farmer who has huge harvesters and tractors. Both the manufacturer and the farmer have to maintain that equipment. Periodically, they check belts and hoses, lubricate parts, properly inflate tires, replace fluids in the hydraulic system, etc. Everything about those systems is checked and rechecked on a regular basis because maintenance is critical for them to succeed in their business.

Now, in many technical fields, there isn't the equivalent of big iron, the big equipment that has to be maintained. So, the maintenance equivalent is your people. The equivalent of the lubricant and checking hoses is ongoing education for your technical staff. Think about it from the standpoint of, "I want to make sure my people are happy and engaged." The bigger issue, the bigger reason, is that by keeping them "maintained," you have a well-oiled "machine" that's going to perform for you at a high level.

Return on Investment

People without access to continuing education can allow that to negatively affect their performance and not work at their highest level. Even beyond personal satisfaction, they put the knowledge they gain from these classes to use in upgrading and enhancing the particular project(s) they're working on. You will update the software or the processes you're using based on their new knowledge.

As you encourage, as you provide continuing education, as you fund those learning opportunities, you let them know you expect them to take seriously this investment you're making in them. That investment creates returns in the form of more efficient work and additional insight employees bring to their jobs, whatever those particular jobs happen to be. The investment made in these employees is returned back four-fold, eight-fold, even twelve-fold relative to what they know, how they can instruct others, and the contacts they make.

Think about the disaster scenarios I've been discussing throughout this book. Potentially in the middle of a disaster, you find yourself needing an expert in a particular field, and one of the developers who you sent to a class happened to be sitting next to someone who knows about that issue. She has the phone number, picks up the phone, calls the expert, and all of sudden she has the necessary insight to solve the problem. How much would it be worth to have access to the right person who could specifically address the issue you had, right at the moment you had it?

Earlier in the book, I talked about a particular problem we experienced at Goldleaf. Ultimately, somebody outside the company who came in and took a fresh look at the problem solved it. Well, the only reason we knew about that specific individual was because one of our senior developers had met him through ongoing education, and they had formed a gathering of people in that industry who went to these additional training classes within the Nashville, Tennessee area. They formed a group that would periodically go have lunch. They might go out and do something fun, shoot pool, or play video games, or whatever.

But they also talked a lot, not necessarily about their individual projects because they were from different companies doing different types of programming, but they talked about the basic development process, tools, techniques, procedures, and the problems they were overcoming. They also shared the tools and tips they were finding that allowed them to be successful within their particular area of expertise.

So, because of that group, one of our developers knew this individual, and we were able to reach out and find him. He came in with a completely fresh set of eyes and looked at things and asked, "What do I see? What is going on here?" And from that perspective, we were able to solve the problem. The point is we knew about that guy because he was a part of a networking situation that one of our senior developers was a part of, and he was a part of that because we encouraged it, we funded it, we sent him off to additional schools, and allowed him to go for long lunches when this group met. By encouraging him in that way, this outside resource became the greatest single element in overcoming that particular problem.

Many managers or business owners reading this chapter may not agree with how I am characterizing the need for removing obstacles. Some see buying additional monitors or massages as "coddling" employees and take a hard line on what might be deemed frivolous activities. But let me wrap up this chapter by asking those that may feel this way to assess what possible downside there would be to trying some of the concepts I am outlining here. Sure it may cost a few bucks, but you should be able to quickly see whether there is any lift in productivity, reduction in turnover, or other similar positive outcome(s).

If you don't see any benefit, you can always revert to your old methods. But if you are serious about taking your business to the next level, and yours is a people-driven enterprise, then focusing on elements that increase job satisfaction or removing obstacles will provide long-term benefits well beyond any (reasonable) monies spent.

Helpful Ports Along the Way

Suppose you had access to a sailboat and you invited a couple of people on a sailing journey. Besides the craft itself, its seaworthiness, and whatever gear and supplies it may already have on board, you still have to consider a few other things before you set off on your journey.

First of all, how long will you be gone? Are you going on a day trip? Are you sailing for a couple of days? A week? A month? Are you trying to sail around the world? All of those options require different types of preparation relative to how many and what types of supplies you need. Even if you're sailing around the world, you cannot store everything you'll need for the entire circumnavigation. You wouldn't have enough space. Consider the route you're taking. Which way are you sailing around the world?

Once you have a basic path, you start examining the ports. Where can I stop to restock? You would look for places that sell the specific supplies you might need en route. Where will you go to repair sails or buy new sails along the way? If you have a problem over this particular stretch of ocean, and you need to get some engine work done, where are the closest ports that offer repairs for your type of engine?

On the path of your journey, you would look for those places where you already know help is available. Of course, the information available to us today is comprehensive compared to what sailors had in the 1860s. But even back in those days, information was available. Sailors talked to each other. They talked about the ports where they had received assistance or restocked supplies. They knew where certain types of craftsmen lived, maybe an expert carpenter or somebody who could work metal or repair sails and so on. They didn't have to worry about diesel engines and GPS navigation, but the situation really isn't significantly different today than it was 150 years ago relative to making sure you have a plan for where you can get help if help is needed.

When you begin your new journey, a new company, or a new product, you should look for the equivalent of ports where you can find some assistance. If you're moving into a new area, you'll be tapping into your family and friends to get recommendations about schools and doctors, etc. You might reach out and make some contacts at the company you're about to join. Set up a phone call and talk with someone who is at the same level of the company as you, asking about the atmosphere in the office. How do people dress? What are the local mores? What's the vibe of the place? What are the managers like? You get a heads-up instead of just coming in cold.

The List

If you have a company that manufactures a product or offers a service, and you're trying to mitigate a future disaster, one of the keys is anticipating the types of things that are more than likely to occur and determining what support would be needed to address those potential events. How do I find the equivalent of the craftsmen in port, a metal worker, a welder, a carpenter or a mechanic to repair mission-critical equipment? How do I get access to those individuals before a disaster actually occurs?

During the major software disaster at Goldleaf, I did not have a list of the different people who could potentially help us from a database management standpoint nor from a code review standpoint. I didn't have the names and numbers of consultants at Microsoft who might be able to provide services relative to the

.NET infrastructure we were using. I didn't know who at Microsoft would be able to specifically advise us relative to the SQL server we were using.

I'm giving you a specific example of our software company, so the resources you would need are probably completely different. You might be a financial institution, a cabinet shop, or a restaurateur. Each company's needs are different. But without having to think too hard, you can likely anticipate the kinds of resources you will need access to. Then, in advance, create a list of reliable resources or consultants you can contact, a special list you keep in your smartphone or as a hot sheet, the equivalent of an emergency numbers list.

Here is a sample list for a software development company. Your list will be different and specific to your type of company, but this should give you an idea of the type of list I am talking about:

Category	Company, Contact, Email Address, Cell Phone, Work Phone, Notes
Network Hardware	
Network Software	
Workstation Hardware	
Workstation Software	
LAN Specialist	
WAN Specialist	
Telecomm	
Production Operating System	
Programming Infrastructure (.Net)	
Programming Language Support	
Programming Language Consultant(s)	
Specialized Software (ie: SAP CRM) Specialist	

Category	Company, Contact, Email Address, Cell Phone, Work Phone, Notes
Database Admin	
Database Consultant(s)	
Outsourced HR Resource	
Outside Accountant	
Outside Counsel	
Company Resource(s) (basically, this is anyone from a company similar to yours that you have formed a relationship with)	

Start this list based on the low-hanging fruit, the things you automatically know you're going to need. If you own a print shop, do you have the names and numbers of multiple people who can fix every critical piece of machinery in your shop? How quickly can you get a repair technician if your mission-critical machine breaks down, making it impossible to print high-revenue jobs? If you only have one name on your list, I don't think you've done all you should to prepare. Do you have multiple suppliers of that specialty ink you use?

Find multiple resources for all mission-critical infrastructure, hardware, software, or services. Included in this category is making sure you have backups to restore all computer systems and continue processing. Let's face it, if you did own a print shop, it's probable that any equipment you operate is run by computers and having access to reliable backups of the software and files used to run print jobs becomes mission-critical for your business. And not just one, but two backups: utilizing the grandfather, father, son approach, just to be sure.

Grandfather/father/son refers to three copies of the data. The son is the data that is actively being used. The father is an incremental backup kept onsite and done frequently, at least daily. Some businesses back up mission critical data hourly. The grandfather is a systemic backup stored offsite in a safe, fireproof location. This backup is done at least weekly. We all know how important backups are; yet without fail, time and time again, many of us don't do it.

Just as the crew from the *Grafton* were faithful for a time to go up every single day and scan the horizon for a rescue ship but then eventually stopped, we take a break from the perseverance needed for success. We say, "I'm really busy. I'll do it soon." Maybe not that day or the next, but one day that will come back to bite you, simply because you weren't diligent about consistently doing everything possible to mitigate or prevent a disaster.

Sources for the List

You will create this list from your own research and from conversations with people who have companies like yours. Read trade journals from your field. Go to conferences where people are discussing the crises they have encountered. Anytime you hear somebody speak about a particular problem and what they did to overcome it, go up to them afterwards and ask them this question: "What resources did you need to have during the disaster that you did not have a resource for in advance?"

If they talk about a particular type of resource they needed, and if that type of resource sounds like something you might need, then later you find one or two resources in that area you can reliably count on in your time of crisis. The specific resource they mention may not directly correlate to your business, but it might spark you to think of a related resource. "Well, I wouldn't need a welder, but I would need access to someone who could repair specialized pottery." Capture whatever those resources are and add it to your list.

Think about your list and how you would go about creating it. Then make sure you have it at hand, so, when something happens, you're neither searching for it nor asking somebody else for it. You know exactly where it is. Before the situation develops into a real problem, you've already reached out to those resources, and you're well on your way to resolving it. It's kind of old-school, but I have a business card portfolio that is specific to all of the people and businesses that I may need to use in a crisis. If my house was burning down, this portfolio is amongst the items designated to be grabbed on my way out the door.

Alerting Your Resources

This brings up another issue. When I talk to people about who to contact in a crisis, I often hear something like, "Well, I'm not sure I want to reach out to {fill in the name of a consultant you might need to use in a crisis} because they're really expensive, and if I don't really need them, I don't want to pay. It might turn out to be nothing."

Say you manage a restaurant at the beginning of a potential crisis. It doesn't look good. It could be a huge problem, or it could be a minor thing, but at that point you don't know. Do you call the restaurant equipment expert on your list? Here's my advice: at a minimum, you contact the expert, and you give her a heads-up. You say, "Hey, I just wanted to alert you. We have the potential for a serious problem here. I don't know if this is anything that will require your services, but I just wanted to find out, over the next forty-eight hours, what's your availability?"

If she says, "Hey, I'm available. Just call me if you need me," then great. Even if you have to contact her early in the morning or late at night, she already knows you have a crisis situation. But she might also say, "I'm leaving for vacation next week," or, "I'm going to be involved in a project out of town, so I'm not available for the next two weeks."

That allows you to move on to your next resource on the list to give them a heads-up, so maybe they can be prepared to help. This is why you have multiple resources lined up for any particular element of the business. Returning to the Goldleaf SQL database example, let's say I ran through all three of those consultants in my initial heads-up call and none were available in the short term. Before I even know I have a big problem on my hands, I now know I need to chase down and find a fourth SQL expert before days go by, before the issue becomes a major meltdown nuclear problem.

Be Willing to Spend Some Money

Give yourself every possible chance for success. Maybe you spend a little money bringing in a consultant, and the issue turns out to be nothing. Lesson learned. The next time something like that happens, and you see it might be the same kind of problem, you can say, "Okay, this is how that other thing started, and it turned out to be nothing." You can take a chance by not giving the consultant a heads-up.

Any money you do spend will keep these consultants at the ready. In other words, they know you're not just crying, "Wolf!" You're a paying customer. So, when you call, they take your call. When you say, "I need your help," they're ready to provide the help. We need to be good stewards of our capital resources, but at the same time we shouldn't let days or even hours go by, missing opportunities to resolve the problem simply because we, as senior executives, senior managers, and individuals, are not willing to spend money to mitigate a problem.

Acquiring Capital, Insurance, and Financial Planning

From here through the end of this chapter, I am going to cover some basic elements of business that I think are crucial for inexperienced business owners and budding entrepreneurs to understand. If you are a seasoned business executive, feel free to skip ahead to the next chapter.

Another aspect of shipping ventures in the 1860s with a modern correlation is acquiring capital funding and insurance. We know Captain Musgrave arranged with his uncle and his uncle's business partner to fund the trip. I think Musgrave felt confident he had secured all the capital he needed. However, by the time they went to buy mission-critical elements, the money had run out. They had to skimp on the all-important anchor chain in length and quality. One has to assume they didn't properly budget this venture. Now, I want to be careful here. I'm not a big fan of sandbagging a project and, by association, sandbagging the budget. I don't think we should go around saying, "Well, whatever we think it's going to cost, double it." Yet, we need to understand a key principle relative to income and expense.

I have to give kudos here to one of my mentors, Bobby Wetherington, who was president of Commercial Banking Company and took a chance on a young, twenty-eight-year-old software programmer, hiring me to come and work at Commercial Banking Company as senior vice-president and placing me on the board of directors. One of the things I learned early on from Bobby was you need to plan for expenses to be more than you expect and for revenue to be less than you expect.

So, when you're preparing your budget, producing all your pro formas and laying out the business plan, you perform a careful analysis, being diligent to calculate what the revenue opportunities are. Consider the possibility that you are being too liberal in terms of those revenue projections. They're too high. Knock them down. You do a similarly thorough job of determining associated expenses. Maybe you carefully calculated what the costs would be, but you weren't aggressive enough. You need to pad those estimates at least another ten to twenty-five percent. If you were extremely conservative on the revenue and extremely aggressive on the expenses, then you can figure out how many months it will take to survive under these premises based on the amount of money you're raising. Again, what I'm telling you here is not rocket science, but I'm amazed that so few of the people going into business following this simple premise.

Let's use some simple numbers as an example. Suppose I start a business that I project will cost about $1000 a month, and I think I can generate $100 in the first month. I think business will ramp up another $50 per month, month two will bring $150 in revenue, month three will bring $200, and so forth. At the same time, some variable expenses will ramp up as we go. If I apply the principle I just mentioned, I would think, "I'm going to cut the revenue projection. I say it's going to take six months before we generate any revenue at all, before we make our first sale. I will also assume it will take me a couple of months of earning $100 before I ramp up to $150 and so forth."

I knock that revenue down, and I bump expenses up. I assume I will need more cash flow than what might be reasonably necessary under this plan to give myself a better-than-even chance for success, because unforeseen things happen. I don't care how good a businessperson you are, unexpected circumstances just happen. I don't care what a good idea you have, something will happen to offset your projections. So, your projections must be modified in order for you to survive.

Raising Capital

Here's the critical part. You need to raise a certain amount of capital. That could come from family and friends or money you already have or money you're borrowing. You take that cash and buy the things you need to start your business. Then you should have a certain amount of cash left over. As you use up that money, you continue to plan with this aggressive expense expectation and extremely conservative revenue expectation. How many months do you have before you run out of money?

Many people attempting a start-up will do these pro formas and say, "Well, hey, we're going to break even in eight months or twelve months." The reality is that a lot of businesses don't break even until well past eighteen months, sometimes even past thirty-six months. If you do a preliminary budget of all likely income and expense, estimate aggressively with the expenses and conservatively with the revenue. If your model shows you break even in six months, good for you. There are obviously businesses that do, in fact, attain cash flow positive status that fast (or faster!). But it's more likely that you're not being realistic about how much your income and expense will actually be. Here's the real key: how much money have you planned for, and does it run out before your spreadsheet says it will run out?

This is the single biggest reason why businesses fail: failure to adequately plan for necessary cash flow. They don't plan for enough capital to start in the first place. You might have an unbelievable idea for a business and run out of money, literally, just two to four months before your business would have become a smashing success. If you realize you're $50,000 short, you have to secure access to that cash, whether you have it in accounts, a line of credit, or from investors who are willing to put up that kind of money.

What typically happens is this: the business is going and things are starting to grow. You're still under water each month, but that's starting to shift. Then you get close to running out of money, and you start to panic. You approach a bank, an investor, family members, or friends. They look at your business, but you're not showing any profitability, even though you're still growing. You look very risky. You look like a business that's about to go under ... because you are. If you don't get that $50,000, you will be out of business. Yes, I realize that I'm sharing some basic accounting concepts.

The key is to secure all of the funding you need up front, that fully funds the venture to a reasonable time to ensure its success. Then you won't need more later. Great! Your business has what it needs to succeed. If you encounter success earlier than projected, you can pay back the investors early. You can pay back your bank loans early. You can return money to family and friends early. Great! Good for you. Better to have that scenario than the alternative: coming with your hat in your hand, explaining why you're in a panic because you didn't plan for how long it would take the business to sustain before it could get to cash flow positive.

Insurance: Buy It before You Need It

The second issue has to do with insurance. A lot of young entrepreneurs don't bother with insurance, like a lot of young individuals. If you're a young professional, you might not have thought much about long-term care. Maybe you're not married yet. Maybe you have no life insurance. If you own a car, you have car insurance because it's required by law. Why do you need life insurance? It's just you. But what happens if you're in an accident and can't work? The thing about insurance is that you never need it ... until you need it.

It's always cheaper to buy it when you don't need it. Long-term care and life insurance is incredibly inexpensive to buy when you're young. So, buy it when you're young and pay for it through the years. When you're older, you have inexpensive insurance because you've been paying into it over the years. Contrast that with waiting to buy insurance until you become forty-five or fifty-five. You either can't get it or it's incredibly expensive. It's painful to see people who are in desperate need of insurance but are past the point of qualifying for it. Truly heart-breaking.

When you think about your preparation for the journey, you're not only thinking about yourself, but also about your spouse, or future spouse. Should you unfortunately pass away, replacing your income might be critically important for your spouse. If you're a business owner and your active involvement is critical to the success of the business, insurance provides money that may allow the business to survive your passing.

This can be a benefit for employees to know that you have planned for this contingency. You want to make sure you have all the different kinds of insurance that would be appropriate, even if in some cases it might seem onerous to you. It might feel like bamboo shoots up your fingernails to buy this insurance because you're convinced it's a waste of money. You might rock through the years, paying for insurance for decades and never need it. But, it's not retroactive. You have to buy it before you need it.

Insurance can be a big part of succession planning. As referenced above, you might consider buying insurance on those individuals who are critical to the success of the enterprise (also known as "key-man" insurance). If you're a small shop or an individual with only a few employees or no other employees, and you want your business to succeed without you, one of the ways to do that is to purchase key man insurance, so money is available to hire somebody with your skills to replace you if something happens.

I frequently ask, "What will happen if you get hit by a bus?" But guess what? People really do get hit by buses. Then, they are not around to shepherd the company to success. Have you left your company in a position to survive even if you don't? Have you left your family in a position to thrive financially? Do you have young children, and will they be able to afford to go to college and pay for weddings? Again, when you're young, it's hard to predict what all those costs will be, yet we have the opportunity to think about those things and properly insure ourselves or our businesses.

If you are in a business with the possibility of generating some kind of liability (and, quite frankly, there are few businesses that don't), then you need professional liability insurance. As a professional speaker, I go out and speak at conferences and share my insight with audiences. What kind of professional liability am I incurring in doing that? You might think none. But I could fall off the stage, injure somebody, and get sued. Stranger things have happened! Somebody could come back and say, "Well, we listened to something you said at the conference, and we tried that approach, but because of that we lost $500,000."

Knock on wood. That's never happened, and I don't expect it to happen. But smart managers insure their companies with commercial insurance products like professional liability, general liability, and E&O (errors and omissions), covering you for something you said or did in error or for liability caused by you omitting critical information. Why? Because we can't control everything. I know what I can control, but I can't control what other people do, so I insure against the potential actions of others.

Think about your funding plan for the venture, for a new project. Do you have all the insurance you need? Just like the good captains back in the 1860s who wanted to make sure they had sufficient capital, insurance, and trip planning, you should desire these things before any business journey you're about to embark on.

Remember, some people make it flying by the seat of their pants. Many more make it by planning for the necessary resources in advance.

CHAPTER ELEVEN
Drifting Towards Disaster

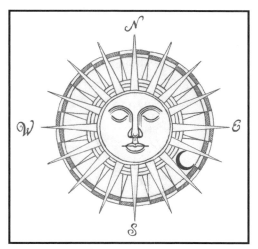

"It is not always what we know or analyzed before we make a decision that makes it a great decision. It is what we do after we make the decision to implement and execute it that makes it a good decision."

— William Pollard

We set a watch, two hours apiece, starting with Dad. I went to sleep below, exhausted but thankful to have finally reached our destination. At 2:00 a.m., Dad woke me for my turn. Instantly awake but not rested, I settled in at the stern and starting gazing at the horizon. It was dark. Whatever small amount of light the moon provided earlier had slipped below the horizon. There was no light by which to read. I found myself nodding off a few times but fought to stay awake until my two-hour shift was complete. However, at some point in the following two hours, the steady rock of the boat and the cumulative exhaustion lulled me back to sleep.

This chapter is focused on decision-making but also addresses the possibility of poor execution on a good decision. We are all familiar with situations where someone, maybe even you, has created a good plan but completely botched the resulting execution of that plan. Maybe your plan was flawless but others executed it poorly (at least that's what we would always tell ourselves in a situation of failure). Let's examine the following matrix of good and bad decision-making juxtaposed with good and bad execution.

	Bad Execution	Good Execution
Good Decision	Sometimes this will work out, but bad execution will often ruin the desired outcome of a good decision.	Best possible outcome. Always strive to achieve this upper right-hand quadrant.
Bad Decision	While this might seem to be the worst possible scenario, sometimes poorly executing on a bad decision can actually lessen the disaster. Still, this is the best of a terrible situation.	Worst possible outcome. While great execution can sometimes lead to positive results, it generally doesn't lessen the negative aspects of the original bad decision.

Staying Awake at the Wheel

So, a good decision with good execution is the optimal scenario. That's the outcome you are striving to achieve. A bad decision with good execution has the potential for serious disaster. I mean, if you've started with a bad decision, and you execute that perfectly, you're in a world of hurt, by definition. Similarly, a good decision with bad execution could be just as disastrous because, even though you've made the right decision, when you execute it badly, you're certainly not going to achieve the right result. Interestingly, the bad decision/bad execution option has the potential to not be the disaster you might expect. Even though the original decision was a bad one, executing it poorly could mitigate the negative aspects of the poor decision, and serendipitously turn out okay. To be clear, I'm not recommending that you use the bad idea/bad execution option as a strategy for success.

If you think about it, out of those four quadrants, only the good decision/good execution provides a likely positive outcome. Therefore, you might think people would spend equal amounts of time coming up with the good decision and making sure execution on that decision is also good. I generally find that not to be the case. I see a lot of time and energy put into making a good decision, particularly from senior decision-makers, but then a lack of diligence to ensure the execution of that good decision occurs.

It could be that decision-makers aren't paying attention. It could be they haven't committed the appropriate resources to make the execution successful. It could be that, once the decision is made, they feel they've done their job, and they assume their staff will execute, yielding a positive result. Any number of things might take an executive's eye off the ball relative to execution, but I've found a more hands-on approach, not micromanaging people but closely supervising them, lets them know I'm still overseeing what's going on, especially in a crisis situation.

Use collaboration with the problem-solving team to develop a detailed execution action plan. Who is going to do what? When will it be done? Are there any tasks that are prerequisites for subsequent tasks, etc. The senior executive assumes responsibility for receiving frequent updates and providing counsel to those working on the specific tasks, and for communicating progress to the overall team while still giving the individuals the "room" to execute the tasks—not micromanagement, but close supervision. Good managers are even more careful to make sure decisions are being executed well because they realize the nature of the disaster, and they've got the CEO looking over their shoulder.

Some people might say, "Hey, that's going to make some people nervous. Let them make the decision and do their jobs." I agree that you need to let people do their jobs and not meddle. But, you also need to provide the appropriate amount of oversight and make sure you are seen, actively managing the execution of this important decision.

In the following stories, I will give examples of when I made a bad decision, when I made a good decision, and the resulting outcomes based on my execution of those decisions.

Near Death on the Eagle River

The first incident I will relate happened to me personally in July of 2014. I was teaching at the Graduate School of Banking at the University of Colorado for two weeks. That left a free weekend in between, so I traveled west up the Rockies to Silverthorne to visit with my good friends, Christine and Andrew Peterson. I love to fly fish and always have great success there. (In my mind, I am an amazing fly fisherman. In reality, I'm just average, so Andrew accommodates my fantasy. Somehow I always fish better when I am fishing with Andrew, imagine that!)

Chris and Andrew had suggested we float the Eagle River. They hadn't fished there in quite a while but heard the fishing might be good. First, we scouted the best place to take out at the end of our journey and arranged for someone to drive Andrew's truck down to that location. We drove to the put-in spot and launched the raft. This was a raft similar to those used for whitewater rafting but with an aluminum fishing frame on top. Andrew was in the middle with a set of oars, Chris was in the back, and I was in the front. We had a wonderful day fishing, stopping along the way to have a nice lunch streamside. We caught a lot of fish! Eventually, we recognized a place close to the take-out spot.

This particular year was a huge snow year, so there was still an extremely high amount of snow melt causing the water to run at a high CFS (cubic feet per second). The water was calmer along the bank, but even a short distance out into the river, the water moved quickly. The place we were taking out was maybe sixty to eighty yards from the start of a series of Class 3 rapids, flowing hard with big, whitewater rooster tails. Where Andrew sat in the middle of the boat, he had access to a lever that released a river anchor, a big, heavy cylinder with spikes coming out of it. It holds the boat in place either in sand or rocks. He got over to the side and dropped the anchor, but the front of the boat was out enough for the current to drag it back toward swift water. The anchor was bouncing along the ground, not able to hold against the force of the water.

Andrew jumped out into ankle deep water. He grabbed the anchor line and pulled the raft closer to shore. I could actually reach out and touch the grass on the bank. Andrew was now about twenty feet behind me, but I could see he was struggling. He was not able to keep the boat from moving forward, so I decided to jump out and hold the front of the boat, which would be enough to keep us from moving forward.

This was my first bad decision.

I assumed I would also be in ankle-deep water, like Andrew. Well, I stepped over the edge and immediately went in over my head. My falling in pushed the raft further out into the current, making it impossible for Andrew to hold the raft, and off it went. Andrew was now by himself, I was free-floating, headed down toward the rapids, and Chris was still in the back seat with no control of the raft, also headed toward Class 3 rapids.

First Instincts Can Be Dangerous

I had not taken my life vest off. A lot of people take their life jackets off when they get near the shore. Had I removed that life jacket, it's very possible I would have died that day because I had to free swim about 150 yards of Class 3 rapids. I've been whitewater rafting a lot and, from that experience, I know you have to get in the swimmer's position—face downstream, head up, with your feet up, so you can fend off rocks. While I had a life vest, I did not have a helmet. I tumbled several times but, by the grace of God, did not hit my head. So, I made it through that first set of rapids and came into calmer water.

I was maybe twenty yards from the shore, and I could have saved myself, but at that moment I looked to my left and saw Chris in the raft. She had moved to the center seat and was trying to maneuver with the oars. She was only about fifteen feet from me, so I made the decision to go to the boat because my instinct was, "Hey, that's my friend Christine. I'm going to help her."

This was my second (and perhaps worst) bad decision.

By swimming to the raft, I pushed myself further out into the faster moving water and wound up putting Chris in additional peril. Chris afterwards told me that she thought she could have navigated to the calm area and made it to shore, but as soon I moved toward her she was concerned she would either whack me with the oar or run over me with the raft. So, she stayed in the rough water. Because of my poor decision, we both went down another hundred yards of white water.

After that stretch, I was able to swim to shore, and nearby, the anchor wedged between some rocks in the middle of a huge rapid, leaving Chris stuck in the middle of the river. Andrew had run all the way down the rocky, uneven shoreline—not an easy task for anyone, but Andrew had not yet fully recovered from breaking his leg in a freak skiing accident earlier that year. Andrew and I reached the place where Chris was stuck, she threw a man overboard rope to Andrew, and he pulled her close enough to the shore to jump on the raft. After assessing there was no way to free the anchor, he cut the anchor line and set the raft free. They floated downriver to a place where they could get to the bank and take out. It all ended okay. I didn't die, Andrew only lost an anchor, Chris got experience in rowing the raft, and we all have a story to talk about.

Looks Can Be Deceiving

Here's my point. If somebody was watching this event unfold and saw I had a chance to go to the raft but saved myself instead, would they have thought of me as a weak leader? Would they have said, "Look at that guy. He left that woman on the boat to fend for herself and just saved himself." It would be difficult for a casual observer of this event not to see the situation that way.

The reality is much different. An absolute tenet of rafting is: If you go overboard and have a chance to get to the bank, you get to the bank. Think of it this way. If I had made it to the raft, what would I do next? A raft sitting idly in the water is extremely difficult to climb into by yourself. Most of the time, you need somebody to grab you by your life jacket and pull you in, so you wind up lying on top of your rescuer. Given the circumstances, it is highly unlikely that Chris at 120 pounds was going to pull me in at 220 pounds.

Going to the raft was a bad decision. That was poor individual leadership.

In this particular example, saving myself would have been the right decision because Chris probably would have saved herself. What if she had gone through the rapids, upended, been injured or, God forbid, killed because of my decision? That result would be almost as bad as what happened with the *Concordia*.

The main difference between what I did and what the *Concordia*'s captain did is intention. My intention was good, but I still made a bad decision. The *Concordia*'s captain didn't make a good decision, and he definitely did not have the right intention. What we do as individuals has to be grounded by the idea of making a disaster situation better, not worse. I will do things that put me in a position to be rescued or be a rescuer, but more importantly I will not do things that actually cause more danger or more harm, even if it might appear to the outside observer that I'm doing something selfishly. So, using all of the information and knowledge I possess, I have to know what I'm doing is good and helpful, then make decisions and exhibit effective leadership relative to that.

Think about this scenario. You're at the office when a fire breaks out at an employee's workstation. The growing flames are beginning to block the employee's escape. Instead of going to the fire, you run to the break room to retrieve the fire blanket stored there, and then go back to the employee and use the blanket to extinguish the fire.

Now, somebody might look at your actions and say, "Why didn't you go help them immediately?"

Going to help them without any reasonable means to deal with the fire might have meant their harm. If you went immediately to their aid, what would you have done? You can't pat the fire out with your hands. Sometimes you make a plan in a time of crisis to provide aid or be a rescuer, and you exhibit good personal leadership, but at the time it doesn't look like you made the good decision. There will always be plenty of time afterwards to say, "This is what my intention was."

Close Call

From an individual perspective, sometimes you need to realize when you're in over your head. Another sailing experience illustrates this point well. On an earlier sailing trip, my dad and I were heading to the Bahamas at night, as was our custom. I was taking my turn at the wheel, and my dad was asleep in the cabin. I kept the *Alacrity* on the specific compass heading and just sailed along. There was no real activity. There was nothing to do or think about. Stay on the right heading. That's it. It was utterly monotonous.

Way, way off in the distance, miles ahead but off to my left, moving from left to right was some type of big vessel, like a container ship. Of course, I couldn't tell for sure from that distance. All I saw were the lights. As I gradually got closer, I noticed there were lights from a much smaller ship in front of it. Each minute brought me closer. It was one of those situations where you can see the boat is moving in front of you, but you're predicting the timing and placement of a potential collision.

I was looking at both vessels, thinking, "They're going to pass in front of me. I'll just stay on my heading, and they'll have passed by the time I sail through their position."

We came closer and closer, and it appeared that I was going pass between these two ships. I decided to sail behind the first vessel, which was, by my estimation, easily a mile in front of the other vessel. From my perspective, I reasoned, "If I turn ninety degrees to go around, that's like an extra thirty minutes waiting for the big ship to pass, and then I have to recalibrate my compass heading. I'm just going to pass right between them."

As we got even closer, something just didn't feel right. The spacing between these two vessels never changed. That was odd. Usually, if you see two vessels out there on the ocean, one's going a different speed, so the distance between them wouldn't remain constant. The closer we came, the two ships never varied in how far apart they were spaced, so the weird feeling strengthened.

I decided to wake Dad up. I said, "Hey, I'm sorry, but this situation just looks weird, and, ya know, I want you to come look at this."

So, he comes out on deck. We're only a couple hundred yards at this point from crossing the line between these two vessels. Dad just stared. He looked at the small boat that had now passed to the right.

He looked back at the huge ship on the left and immediately shouted, "Cable!"

He grabbed the wheel and spun it extremely hard to port. Slowly at first but steadily, we veered off. We wound up sailing quite close, parallel to the second vessel, which turned out to be an enormous barge. Even in the dark, as we got closer, I could see the massive, steel cable, maybe six inches in diameter, connecting that barge to a huge oversized tugboat, nearly a mile in front, towing this barge in the open ocean. It was something you might see on the Mississippi River. It was unusual (for me at least) to see that out in the open Atlantic.

If I had continued on the same course and run into that cable, it would have torn straight through the sailboat. It would have completely shredded masts, shrouds, and lines. Maybe even my head! Everything would have been gone. That truly would have been a disaster.

This was a situation where I wanted to make the big decision by myself. But you know what? I was not confident enough that making the decision would be in the best interest of me or my dad or the boat. I needed to seek help to get the information I needed to make sure this was a good decision. By going to my more experienced father for advice, I completely averted a disaster. This is an example where I made a good decision (to seek out my dad's advice) and executed that well. My dad made a good decision to avoid plowing straight ahead and getting torn up. He executed that decision well.

Sailing in between the tugboat and the barge would have been a bad decision. At the time, I considered it a good decision because I didn't know about the cable. I was not including the worst-case scenario. As we learned from Chapter 9, if I had considered the possibilities of crashing our sailboat into one of the vessels or hitting a tow cable, the decision to delay our trip by thirty minutes would have been a no-brainer. The error was in not knowing and not understanding the lighting system on the two boats.

The lighting pattern indicated it was a towed barge. If I had been more aware of the position of the lights, I wouldn't have even come that close. I would have known there was a huge tow cable between them because of the way they're required to run those lights at night. We never would have come close to a panic situation.

Good decision/bad decision and good execution/bad execution combine to determine how a decision will turn out. Out of those four quadrants, the good decision paired with good execution is the only one that leads to a likely positive result.

CHAPTER TWELVE
The Mistakes

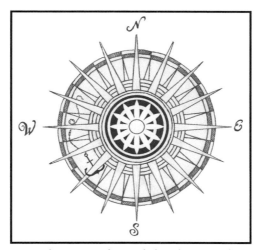

"For the want of a nail the shoe was lost,
For the want of a shoe the horse was lost,
For the want of a horse the rider was lost,
For the want of a rider the battle was lost,
For the want of a battle the kingdom was lost.
And all for the want of a horseshoe nail."

— Benjamin Franklin

Experience is the best teacher. Once you've gone through a crisis, you learn from that. Those memories, particularly the ones where the crisis was extremely strong or personal, motivate you to respond differently next time. Some of you reading this book have never had a serious emergency. You may have no plans to proactively prepare for disasters as I've advocated in this book.

To you, I would say, "You must." Especially if you're in any kind of leadership position, you have to override your natural inclination toward inertia. You must absorb the most helpful elements from these chapters and utilize them. Be sure you have the right kind of resources and the right team members. Be sure you have given yourself every possible chance for mitigating a disaster, even if you have no experience with disaster to instruct you. If there are x number of things that will be helpful in a disaster, you might only be able to anticipate fifty percent of those or possibly seventy-five percent. But, trust me, even if you only accomplish half of the preparation you could, you will be significantly better off, either toward resolving a potential crisis situation quickly or significantly mitigating the negative effects of a crisis because of your preparation.

When researching the wrecks of the *Grafton* and *Invercauld*, it struck me that both of the wrecks could have been likely avoided based on the captain's decisions related to the anchors. An anchor is an inanimate object. By itself, it cannot be positive or negative. It just sits on the deck of a ship. In order for the anchor to be useful at all, it needs to be in a position to be useful immediately. The anchor needs to be firmly attached to the anchor chain. The chain needs to be firmly attached to the anchor line. The anchor line must be firmly attached to the ship.

Now, I realize that all of this sounds obvious, but you would be surprised at how many boats are put into peril simply because the anchor is not firmly attached. So, if the anchor is ready for use and the captain calls for the anchor to be lowered, then the crew must be able to access the anchor and follow the orders. This includes a situation where it may be pitch black with raging seas, howling winds, and freezing conditions. Separately from following an order to lower the anchor, any seaman might instinctively utilize the anchor based on knowledge and training for when it is appropriate to use the anchor to save the ship. A ready-for-use anchor, a crew that knows how to deploy it, and a captain that knows when to deploy it all factor into the positive aspects of having an anchor hold the ship fast and out of danger.

The *Grafton* sailed on its journey with a fatal flaw sitting on its deck. The anchor itself was fine and perfectly capable of holding the ship in a storm. But due to a lack of funds and poor planning for how provisions were acquired, Captain Musgrave only had 180 feet of chain on board to serve two anchors. As previously referenced in Chapter 10, that amount of chain only allowed them to safely anchor in less than twenty feet of water! Not only was the length of chain not nearly enough, the quality of chain was substandard, meaning that, in a storm, the links of the chain itself may not be sufficient to hold the ship.

During the storm that forced the *Grafton* toward the coast of Auckland Island, Captain Musgrave properly gave the order to lower the anchor. The crew properly followed the order to lower the anchor. But the water depth was too deep for the anchor to effectively hold the ship fast. By the time the anchor did catch, the storm was blowing so hard that the chain gave way and the ship was doomed to the rocks.

The *Invercauld* had a different situation with its anchor, but met the same fate. Upon leaving Australia, bound for South America to pick up a load of fertilizer (yuck), there was no expectation of encountering any land. As the South Pacific can be quite a rough ride, Captain Dalgarno ordered the anchor to be lashed to the deck, eliminating the possibility of it sliding around in rough seas. When the *Invercauld* encountered the Aucklands, it was at night.

Confused over which of the islands he was encountering, Dalgarno made an error by turning into the island instead of away from it. Once the magnitude of that error was realized, the only option to save the ship was to use the anchor to hold the ship in position. However, the anchor was lashed to the deck! In the dark, the sailors were unable to free it in time to throw it overboard. Without any means of stopping their forward progress toward the rocks, the ship was doomed.

Two anchors. Two mistakes by two captains. Two shipwrecks. It's easy to look back in hindsight and say what would have happened. It's possible that both the *Grafton* and the *Invercauld* would have shipwrecked regardless of the decisions by the two captains on the use of their respective anchors. But we can say with some certainty that it is likely both the *Grafton* and *Invercauld* could have been saved had their respective anchors been ready to use and actually effective when used.

Perhaps neither Musgrave nor Dalgarno had ever had a situation like this one ever occur, so they had no direct experience with it. Unlikely, but possible. Even if they had not personally had this type of event occur, every captain knows that having an anchor at the ready and usable at a moment's notice is a must. So, there is no excuse for their errors regarding the anchors.

Anatomy of a Mistake

Mistake. That is a heavy word. The definition of mistake as a noun includes this: an action or judgment that is misguided or wrong. There are two types of mistakes that the definition codifies: something that turns out to be wrong and something that is misguided. Another way to interpret this definition is that one is likely inadvertent, and the other is purposeful. Regardless of how long you have walked this planet or had a professional career, you have made mistakes.

Think of the types of mistakes you have made. You can probably separate past mistakes into the two categories easily. Think of the times that you moved forward with an action plan that turned out to be wrong. It can be as simple as thinking that the Beta format of videotape would win out over VHS.[8] Or you could have decided that purchasing a newly created machine would add value to your manufacturing business. A decision that in and of itself cannot be deemed to be faulty at the time can in fact turn out to be wrong and subsequently be called a mistake. The machine worked fine but something changed in your industry and made the equipment obsolete. You might even say, "Buying that machine was a mistake," without indicating that your reasoning in buying it was in error.

Contrast that with the other form of a mistake, one that is misguided. Misguided indicates that there was fault with your judgment or reasoning. These mistakes are usually bigger, more damaging and, if done consistently, without remediation, can lead your crew to abandon ship. Using the machine example from above, if you had asked someone knowledgeable in your industry, and they had informed you that changes were likely coming that would make the equipment obsolete, then your misguided purchase of that piece of equipment is an avoidable error in judgment. Making mistakes that are well-meaning but turn out to be wrong are inevitable. Minimizing misguided mistakes is imperative.

Anatomy of an Apology

Another way to see the difference between the two types of mistakes is to examine the type of apology that is associated with each type of mistake. When you make an inadvertent mistake, like

8 For you Millennials, Beta was a superior format of videotape that battled the VHS format for dominance of the video market pre-DVDs. VHS won running away, only to be replaced by shiny round disks....

making a wrong turn and showing up late to an appointment or you dropping a glass that breaks, you might say, "My bad," or, "I'm sorry." Your apology is heartfelt, but it's not that big of a deal. The error was not intentional and, in the big scheme of things, it's not that important and the negative impact is small.

Contrast that with a misguided mistake. You have committed an egregious offense, like specifically driving down a one-way street thinking you can beat oncoming traffic to a driveway, but crashing into a car. Your specific action was not an inadvertent mistake; you knowingly made the illegal turn. Or consider a misguided mistake of omission, like forgetting your spouse's birthday or your wedding anniversary. Before you say, "That's not that big of a deal," consider that the emotional harm you can cause by not keeping track of important dates can hurt someone just as sure as a car accident.

In either case, your apology would need to be more, not just a "my bad," but a sincere apology recognizing your specific action (or omission) that caused the mistake and asking for forgiveness. Note that a key element for this type of apology is the conscious omission of any excuse for the mistake. For example, if you say, "I am so sorry for not remembering your birthday. It was totally stupid of me to do that, but it was because I have been so busy with work…." Any apology that comes with additional reasoning negates the healing impact of the apology.

When you make a mistake, just own up to it. Don't offer excuses. There will be time later for explanations, if appropriate. This is especially important for leaders; you are not infallible and, trust me, your employees know it. So, when you make a mistake, give a heartfelt apology and, if necessary, ask for forgiveness. Then work to avoid future mistakes of that type. I've found that my employees always gave me a lot of grace when I admitted mistakes, but that well is not deep. Continuing to make the same types of mistakes will indicate that you are not willing or able to learn from your mistakes.

Mistakes of Execution Versus Innovation

One other distinction I would make about mistakes is the difference between a mistake in execution and a mistake in innovation. We tend to think of mistakes as all bad, but that is not true at all. When we are inventing, trying new things, there are going to be mistakes. And these are actually important; we learn about what is not a good solution and can iterate toward a successful outcome.

Mistakes are bad when they are avoidable and repeated. I have worked for nearly my whole business career in financial services and spend a lot of time with bank and credit union personnel. The person you interact with most often in a financial institution branch traditionally is the teller. A teller interacts with customers or members all day long, performing transactions and handling cash and other negotiable documents (like checks or share drafts). At the end of the day, they must balance their drawer and hopefully not be over or under the amount of cash that the computer says should be in the drawer.[9]

A teller that frequently has a drawer out of balance is making an error in execution and, if not quickly remediated, will find themselves looking for a new job. However, say that teller is attempting to assist a customer and goes a bit off script in their attempt to provide great customer service, yet what they actually did runs afoul of banking regulations. While they need to understand what the rules are and how to follow proper procedures the next time, they should not be chastised or punished. Their intention was to help a customer and their error in innovation should not be squelched. For if you do, you will create a staff of robots, who mindlessly follow a narrow set of instructions and have learned to never stray from the script. What a shame it would be if that occurred.

---

9 Believe it or not, financial institutions are just as upset over having too much cash in the drawer than not enough, perhaps more so. Too much cash indicates that one or more customers were cheated in a transaction during the day with no way to know who or how much.

— David L. Peterson —

Get Your Anchors Ready

I'm encouraging you in this book, and I'm encouraging you in this chapter: think through the things you can do today or this week to prepare yourself or your company for a disaster and avoid mistakes.

What are the equivalents, for your business, to having usable anchors at the ready? It might be setting up an automatic maintenance routine like creating a backup or keeping a list handy of the resources you might need in a crisis (two or three people/resources for each area of potential crisis, according to your unique situation).

Sit yourself down and think, or meet with your senior leaders or other people in your industry who have more experience than you. Come up with a list of those mission critical areas that, in a pinch, you need to be able to access and tap resources that can assist in mitigating a disaster and resolving it quickly. Make sure you have the right group of mature, confident people with you who will all be useful in solving a crisis, who will keep a level head, and who have the requisite amount of experience, particularly in intangible skills, that may be critical in a disaster.

Be the kind of leader who earns the respect of your employees, co-workers, and friends, who would recognize that your level-headed decision-making and strategic, benevolent leadership makes you worth following.

Many of you will read this book and agree these are good ideas and things you should do, and yet you won't do them. You won't do them! You'll delay and put it off until something traumatic happens, and then you'll despair and agonize over your procrastination. I implore you to do every possible, reasonable thing you can do in advance to mitigate disaster.

CHAPTER THIRTEEN

Grounding the *Alacrity*

*"Life is a shipwreck, but we must not forget
to sing in the lifeboats."*

— Voltaire

*I was instantly awake. Something wasn't right. I realized I had fallen
asleep and was frantically looking around. I saw nothing. The night
was totally dark. But then I felt it. A soft thumping that shook the
whole boat.*

What was that?

Then it hit me. It was the keel hitting the bottom! My heart sank, and I immediately rushed below to wake up my dad.

"We are hitting the bottom!" I shouted.

He quickly came out on deck and made a quick sweep, assessing the situation.

My friend, Vince, came out on deck and immediately began asking, "What's happening?"

I ignored him, waiting for Dad to issue a command. He went below to start our ancient diesel engine. It was always difficult, like trying to start a lawn mower that had rotted in a shed for ten years. He turned the crank on the flywheel again and again. The old thing would not turn over.

The waves were relentless. Each minute that passed, the Alacrity was pushed farther onto what turned out to be a coral reef.

At this point, Vince lost control, succumbing to the fear we all felt. He started yelling, screaming, "Help! Help! We're going to die! Oh, my God!"

He flailed. He grabbed his head in desperation. He absolutely freaked out. We tried to talk to him, to calm him down, but it was no use. Dad had the idea to get into the dinghy, row out to deeper water and drop the anchor to at least stop the boat from drifting any closer. Our wooden dinghy was big, about ten feet long, and very heavy.

Vince was of no use, so I hauled on the dinghy line by myself. It seemed unusually heavy. When the dinghy was close enough for me to see it more clearly, I realized it was nearly full of water! There had been no rain or heavy seas, so I couldn't imagine how the water got in there. There was no way I could bail out all the water and row to deep water in time by myself. The ship began to tilt and moving around became more difficult.

At last, I heard the old engine turn over!

My heart sank again, though, when I realized the boat had tilted so far toward the cay that the propeller was spinning in the air! We weren't going anywhere using the motor. The waves relentlessly picked up the Alacrity *and pounded her farther onto the reef. She continued to lean until, finally, she heaved over on her side, the tall mast lying right onto the sandy beach of the cay.*

At this point in the story, every wave was picking us up and pushing us further and further inland. Looking back on the events of that early morning, I think this was a great illustration of the question: "Do you continue down a certain path that possibly leads to the best execution, the best solution, or do you abandon a plan that doesn't seem to be working and move on to something else?"

Let's examine this concept in light of the issues facing us that morning. There were four things happening during the crisis that either created a problem or prevented a positive resolution: the engine wouldn't start, the dinghy was full of water, my friend Vince was totally freaking out, and the night was pitch black. Of those four, the engine not starting was the most critical.

Even though Vince had completely and totally lost control of himself, if we had been able to start the engine, we would have been able to stop our forward progress. We could have maneuvered the boat and motored out of trouble. End of story. We would have said, "Oh, my gosh! What a near disaster we had," but it would not have been the actual disaster that ultimately occurred.

Remember, we're in this old sailboat with a very old diesel engine. It was finicky. Once you had it going, it would run forever, but to get this thing started took a lot of effort. You had to manually hand crank a large flywheel to generate compression in order to start it. It was stubborn under the best of circumstances. So, as soon as we became aware of the danger we were in, Dad's first thought was to start the engine. We worked on that immediately, but our attention diverted to Vince. I went to calm him down, but Dad needed my help with the engine. After six or seven attempts, Dad made the decision to try something else to stop the boat's forward progress.

The Third Anchor

If you're headed toward disaster, if possible, think of something you can do that will allow you to avoid complete disaster, something that will stop the forward momentum. You already know that the fates of the *Grafton* and the *Invercauld* could have changed dramatically if their two anchors had been usable and available.

On the *Alacrity*, the issue was, "We have a chance to start this engine, but every second that we don't get it started, we're slowly creeping closer and closer to this island. Eventually, we're going to be so stuck that it doesn't matter if we get the engine started because we'll be past the point of no return."

What can you do to stop sliding further into danger? Think about a car sliding toward a big sinkhole. You can see the hole. You know if you go any further, you're going to fall into it, but you can avoid it if you move quickly enough. If you can position yourself where you're not going to slide further into danger, then it makes sense for you to do that and make every effort to do that.

One possible way to keep us from grounding would have been to get the anchor overboard and secured, stopping our forward progress toward the island. The boat was moving bow-first toward the land, and the anchor was stowed at the bow. If we had put the anchor overboard, then we would have drifted all that distance plus the distance of the length of anchor line. At the very moment I realized we were beginning to touch bottom, if I had gone forward and thrown the anchor out with fifty feet of line, we would have only gone fifty feet and stopped. That would have been a solid, immediate stop to our progress toward the cay and the hull-breaking coral beneath it. Immediately throwing the anchor out would have been a good decision because anything else we tried—starting the engine, being able to access and use the dinghy, and so on—would not have been lessened or muted by the fact that the anchor was out. If the anchor was out and stopped our forward progress, we could have worked for however long it took to get the engine started, then motored out of danger, raised the anchor and gone on our way.

My dad was asleep, and I was in charge of the *Alacrity*, in effect the captain, standing in for my dad while he rested. Unfortunately, I did not have the clarity of forethought at the time. I had not known of the stories of the *Grafton* or *Invercauld* and their fates related to misuse of the anchor. My dad and I did not have any specific drills or discussion about what to do in case the boat began drifting toward an island and you didn't have the engine available to navigate.

Nevertheless, one thing remains true: in case of emergency, stop your forward progress toward disaster! The key lesson here is, had we considered running aground as a possible outcome, we would have discussed the actions to take in order of priority, including dropping the anchor overboard to stop forward progress. In addition, it was something one person could do alone. That was something I could have done to change the outcome of this particular disaster. But I didn't do that. Thus, I add my bad decision, my mistake, to those of Musgrave and Dalgarno regarding the use of the anchor. Three anchors. Three bad decisions by three captains. Three ships grounded.

Plan B Fails

So, after Dad had tried for some time to get the engine started without success, he decided we needed to grab the anchor from the bow, put it in the dinghy and row out behind the stern away from the island. Once it was a fair distance away, we would drop it and secure it, thus stopping any further movement toward the cay. That was a good idea. That was definitely something we could do.

Now, the dinghy was not a newer model, rubber pontoon boat with an outboard engine like you might see on today's luxury sailboats. Our dinghy was big, old, and heavy, a double bow vessel, pointed on both ends, with long awkward oars and oarlocks. It trailed behind the boat on a painter. (For those of you not nautically inclined, a painter is a line or rope that attaches a towed boat. Sailing is full of words that may sound foreign. How does "towrope" become "painter"? The origin of the word appears to be the French word *pentoir* (pen'twa), which means cordage for hanging.)

Picture of my mom (so beautiful!)
with the dingy trailing behind *Alacrity*
—Laure Peterson Collection—

Again, it was dark, so as I struggled with the weight of the dinghy, I wondered why it seemed heavier than usual. Once it was near, I could see it was more than half full of water. I didn't expect that since there had been no rain and no rough seas. Maybe because we were closer to these islands, some waves broke over the sides of the dinghy. We always trailed this dinghy behind us wherever we went. Even when it poured down rain, you could get in it with a bucket and quickly bail almost all the water out. Now, at this critical moment of need, it was half full of water and rendered useless. There was no value whatsoever to this dinghy because, if I had stepped inside at that point, it would have sunk right to the bottom.

Because of the weight of this dinghy, two people would have had to get into the water and try to turn it over. Based on the action of the waves, the fact that it was dark, and the bottom was four and a half feet down and full of sharp coral, I don't think we could have done it if we tried. The moment we realized it was nearly full of water, we abandoned that plan and went back to working on the engine. That was a good decision.

Rule Out Non-Viable Options Quickly

Here's a thought. What if, instead of even fooling with the dinghy, we had continued working on the engine and ultimately started it sooner? Would that have made a difference? We spent a good five minutes thinking about how we could use the dinghy and then deciding a way to bail it out. After we went back to work on the engine, we were ultimately able to get it started. Abandoning the dinghy and returning to the engine was a good decision. But during the time we spent trying to make the dinghy work, the *Alacrity* had moved so far up the slope toward the cay where the water was increasingly shallow that, by the time the engine started, the prop was out of the water. The prop was turning, but it was spinning in the air. Not good!

So, the engine became useless. Really, after that, we were done. Any further effort on our part to save our boat was futile. But, what if, instead of messing with the dinghy, we devoted our energy to the engine and were able to get it started before we had drifted so close to the island that the prop was spinning in the air?

These are easy questions to ask now. This is simple to figure out in hindsight, right? Yeah, of course, hindsight is 20/20. We know what we coulda, shoulda, woulda done at that point by looking back at all the options and how the decisions we did make turned out. The real key is this: how do you make informed decisions in the middle of a crisis that allow you to evaluate the best options for action? Do I spend more time doing activity x, or should I do something else? Because the flip side could equally have been true. We could have worked on the engine wholeheartedly without distraction, and it never started. In that case, had the dinghy not been full of water or had we put the anchor out right away and stopped our forward progress, then those would have been better first options.

The proper order of decision-making should have been:

1. *Immediately* realize we're in trouble and throw the anchor over the side. I didn't do that.

2. *Immediately* check the dinghy to see if it was in working order, take the anchor out, and stop our forward progress toward disaster. We could have done that but didn't.

A Handy Checklist

Let's consider another quick point about the dinghy and disaster preparedness. When we were under sail, we kept the dinghy trailing behind for at least the length of the sailboat, about forty feet. However, once we stopped moving and were just drifting with the sea anchor out, we should have pulled in the painter and tied the dinghy up close to the stern of the *Alacrity*. That way, in the event of an emergency, the dinghy would be immediately at hand and useful. We didn't do that. Maybe we were just overtired. I don't remember us having any conversation about the dinghy once we started drifting.

The key is that, when you have an opportunity to pursue steps in advance of a crisis that will likely have a mitigating effect, you must execute on those steps. I know many experienced sailors who have written checklists for certain events: before departing, when anchoring, upon return, etc. They create laminated documents and walk through the checklists. They may have done this action a thousand times before and probably know the checklist by heart, yet they still follow the checklist. Why? To ensure they execute on every one of the steps, not missing any, and execute steps in the proper order.

Had we had such a checklist, even late at night, we would have pulled the dinghy in close. Now, the question is, "Would that have prevented the dinghy from filling up with water?" It's possible, since being tied up close could have prevented some of the side-to-side motion. But, even assuming that it wouldn't have mattered, and the dinghy was going to be half-full regardless, it would have been so close that we would have immediately seen it was swamped and not useful, saving three to four minutes … which may have made all the difference.

In researching the events of the *Alacrity* shipwreck for this book, I spent some time thinking about that night we ran aground and how I could have executed better. Today, you can buy a device that clips to a hat and sounds an alarm if your head tilts too far (i.e., because you have fallen asleep). There are smartphones that provide entertainment. But these options weren't available back in 1979.

I was discussing this with my dad and he made this comment: "It's possible that even if you had stayed awake, we still would have wrecked the boat." I was initially stunned! Was he giving me a way out of the shipwreck being my fault? But after further analysis, I see he is correct. There was no way for me to know my relative position in the water. It was dark—pitch black. So, even if awake, I wouldn't have any reason to believe that we were headed for danger. On the other hand, had I been awake, I would have had some time, maybe multiple minutes of additional time, to wake up Dad and start working on a resolution a whole lot sooner.

Right now you're probably thinking, "Well, sure, David. If you know everything that's happened already, you can go back and say, 'Yeah, this was the right decision.'" I realize the aforementioned counterfactual reasoning comes into play when you go back and reconstruct different alternative scenarios to live events that have already occurred. But we don't know what would have happened. I'm fairly confident that, even if I had not fallen asleep, we would have drifted toward that island. But, because it was so dark,

I couldn't see the island at all.

However, I certainly would have been aware of impending danger way earlier, giving us much more time to deal with it. But, if I hadn't fallen asleep, would anything have been different? Is it possible that I could have stayed awake and nothing would have changed in the ultimate outcome of the shipwreck of the *Alacrity*? I have to admit the answer is, "Yes." It's very possible that the *Alacrity* was doomed no matter what I did.[10]

In Chapter 6, I addressed how you choose your "crew," but I want to make a few additional comments here. Why is carefully choosing your team so important?

In the case of the *Alacrity*, because Vince was an inexperienced sailor, having never been on a sailboat ever, he was not prepared for what happened. We had a crewmember that not only was not helpful, but also was unintentionally keeping my dad and me from fully focusing on a solution.

For example, we could have been working on the engine while Vince pulled in the dinghy. His unfortunate reaction made it take longer for us to get some things done due to our concern for him. Somebody might not necessarily be helpful, but not necessarily be a hindrance either. They're neutral. They're not helping, but they're not hurting. At a minimum, if you have somebody who's not helping, he needs to be neutral. Frankly, I believe Vince was not prepared to handle any crisis situation.

In hindsight, we could have done a couple of things. We knew for months he was going with us on this sailing trip. We could have taken him out on a couple of Saturday day trips and allowed him to acclimate to the boat and the water, spend some time sailing around off the coast of Florida.

I've asked myself over the years, "Why didn't we do more sailing with him?"

---

10 Whenever I talk about the wreck of the *Alacrity*, I am very clear that I fell asleep as we drifted into the island, and thus the wreck was a direct result of my failure to execute my watch and stay alert.

And then I think, "Holy cow! He was on the boat with us from ten o'clock the night before, all through the next day, and beyond." The sailing we could have done before this trip would not have been more than the amount of sailing he did with us until the point we wound up wrecking the boat. Any amount of day-trip sailing would likely not have prepared him in any way, shape, or form for being a part of a shipwreck. However, we certainly could have talked about some things.

Give a "Prep" Talk

We never even discussed safety precautions in the event of an emergency, other than the location of the life vests. If you charter a sailboat for an afternoon sail, the rental company will go through a ten-minute safety speech, including instructions about life vests and safety procedures. But here we were, an experienced sailor (me) and a more experienced captain (my dad), and we never had any discussion whatsoever about what might happen and what we would do if that happened.

How different would things have been if we had taken the time to make sure Vince understood and knew what would happen in certain situations? "If this happens, this is what we're going to do. David, here's what your responsibility will be. Vince, here's what your responsibility will be. Here's where the life jackets are. Here's what I want you to do." Maybe that is one thing you can easily do in your business: have the equivalent of a fire drill, just so your people have a better shot at not freaking out if something were to actually happen.

Preparing people for how they are going to act in a certain situation is certainly something you can do, and should do, even if you don't know what the disaster is going to be. But, even if you haven't done any of this prep work, you can still maintain control of yourself and encourage those with you to control themselves.

Respond Versus React

In the middle of a crisis, you can choose to respond or react to what's happening. Let me give an illustration from Kairos, which is a Christian-based prison ministry. Over the course of four days, people from the local community go into a prison and provide a retreat for inmates. One of the talks given by a Kairos team member emphasizes the difference between a reaction and a response.

In fact, poor decisions in the moment of choice are precisely what have led to many inmates ending up in prison. They reacted to a situation in which they found themselves rather than taking the time to consider a response. When you react to something, it's usually immediate and without contemplation. Someone hits you; you react and hit them back. The concept of a response centers on an attitude of careful evaluation of the situation. It's a thoughtful reply, requiring you to think about a variety of options you might do or say in response. You take into account all of the external variables, perhaps think about the ways that another person involved in the situation might process information, and evaluate your action choice based on what you feel would yield the best possible desirable outcome. Then, you put your choice into action as opposed to knee-jerk reacting.

Most importantly, when you think through a response, you are considering possible outcomes to your response. When you react to an event, you get what you get. You're not thinking about the impact of your reaction. Whatever happens, happens. But, when you respond to an event, you have a better chance to achieve the outcome you desire. Vince reacted … and it turned out badly.

The Only Thing You Can Control

Choosing how you respond can be vital. Many years ago, during WWII, there was a group of Jews in a concentration camp led by a man named Viktor Frankl, and they decided they were going to control how they responded to the Nazi guards who were hurting all of them. They agreed that, during every injustice, no matter what happened, they would respond with kindness. Every mean act, every ugliness, every hateful, spiteful atrocity, would be met with kindness and love.

Of course, when they started doing this, the guards heaped *more* abuse on them, and they suffered horribly. They acknowledged that the Nazis controlled every aspect of their lives, but the Nazis could not control how they *responded* to any given situation. That was what the prisoners owned. That was the only thing they controlled, and because they controlled that, mentally, they hung on to that. This was their choice. This is what they had freedom to do, and nobody could take this choice away from them. Amazingly, every person in the group, every single one who was practicing this choice of responding to hate with love and caring, survived.

Carefully thinking about how we're going to respond in a situation is a concept that some people seem to innately understand, and other people don't. So, if you are somebody who is more prone to reacting than responding, what would it take for you to start thinking and carefully responding to your spouse, to your parents, to your boss, or to your professor? Insert whomever you have trouble interacting with. How do you shift from reaction to response? It starts by *thinking*. You're thinking now.

Have you ever had a parent or a friend say something like, "You should count to ten before you say anything"? Well, what's the purpose of that? During those ten seconds, you should actually think. It's likely that if you think, even for *ten seconds*, your response might be vastly different than what your immediate reaction would have been to whatever event happened. So, this idea of literally pausing and thinking before you respond is the first step toward changing from a reaction to a response. The outcome isn't 100% guaranteed. There are people who, even if they thought through a response, are still going to act like a jerk or be an idiot. You can't control what anyone else's actions or reactions are, but you can control your response to any given situation.

CHAPTER FOURTEEN
The Rescue

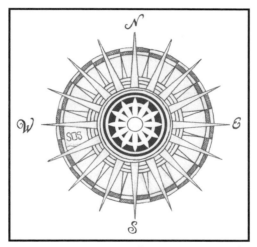

"Patience, persistence and perspiration make an
unbeatable combination for success."

— Napoleon Hill

I find the juxtaposition of how the crews were rescued from the *Invercauld* and the *Grafton* quite fascinating. Dalgarno on the *Invercauld* was headed to South America and not planning to stop at the Auckland Islands. Since they had no expectation of being wrecked on these islands, they had no expectation that anyone would come looking for them. The *Grafton* was a different story.

Survival Mode

Before he left, Raynal insisted on the assurance from Uncle Musgrave and Sarpy that, if the ship didn't return after four months, the investors would alert the government, which would hopefully mount a rescue. Since the *Grafton* left Sydney in November, the crew assumed they would see a boat sometime after March.

The fact that any rescuers who did venture out would head straight to Campbell Island, the crew's original destination, did not lessen their anticipation of being rescued. Raynal and Musgrave determined that, if the rescuers went to Campbell Island and didn't find them there, they would almost certainly swing by and search at Auckland Island because of the proximity of the two island groups. Maybe that's why they immediately went into survival mode for the next four to five months. They were stuck on this desolate island with horrible, biting flies and harsh weather, but all they had to do was survive until the promised rescue ship arrived. Since they expected a rescue ship would be sent specifically to look for them, they did not immediately set up a systematic way to alert passing ships. No signal flag. No bonfire ready to be lit. No posted watch to scan the seas.

Lessons from Hurricane Katrina

Probably the closest comparison most of us might experience to what the *Grafton* and *Invercauld* crews experienced is if we were in the middle of a natural disaster, such as a flood, earthquake, tornado, or hurricane. In August of 2015, the tenth anniversary of Hurricane Katrina, there were numerous features running on TV, showing how the city had fared in the ten years since the devastation that occurred in 2005. Of course, people were reliving the events that led up to the tragedy that occurred in the aftermath of Katrina.

Most people think the hurricane hit New Orleans and caused the bulk of the damage when, in fact, the hurricane bypassed New Orleans and unleashed its fury on the Mississippi coast. I distinctly remember being up early that morning and listening to news reports that "New Orleans has dodged a bullet." What happened next is well-known. Levees and pumping stations that should have protected the below-sea-level city from massive Lake Pontchartrain, failed. There was significant loss of life and property destruction that exceeded $100 billion.

Government agencies were ineffective in dealing with the crisis, and many people were left to fend for themselves. From this crisis arose amazing stories of daring rescues with one consistent thread: nearly all the people rescued had placed themselves in a position of being rescued. Helicopters and boats were rescuing people who climbed on their roofs.

A significant number of the 1,400 people who perished were in their homes, and in most cases a part of the home that was not flooded. They died due to dehydration, heat stroke, heart attack, or lack of needed medicine. Most were elderly. They were not in a position to be rescued, and as a result perished.

We can learn some important lessons from this tragedy:

- **Don't get into a position where you need to be rescued.** Well, hello. Thanks, Captain Obvious! As if we didn't know that. But there were calls for people in the areas around the levees in New Orleans to evacuate, and most people ignored them. They had waited out hurricanes before. This was only a Category 3 storm, so what's the big deal? If you have the chance to move away from a place with a reasonable chance of danger to a place with a reasonable expectation of safety, do it. It doesn't matter how many times it turned out to be a false alarm in the past. You never had to be rescued from any of those events, and you didn't die. That is a successful strategy!

- **When a rescue option comes along, take it.** The residents of Louisiana are amazing people. Many people from the southwest part of the state, only slightly affected by the storm, came in with their boats and rescued people—citizens helping fellow citizens. What if you were on the roof and the water is rising around you? A Cajun fisherman comes around in a boat and says, "Jump in the boat." You say you just talked with the sheriff's department, and they're coming with a helicopter to extract you. You'll wait for them. That's crazy. Anything could happen to delay the helicopter, including the strong likelihood it will be diverted to someone in greater need. When a rescue opportunity is presented, grab it.

- **Be resourceful.** Thinking through how bad the situation might become can help you make choices about how to be rescued before things get out of hand. I'm sure a significant number of people in the flooded areas went to the second floor when the water reached a certain level in their homes. Some saw water coming above the second floor level and moved into their attics. Then they were stuck. They couldn't retreat; they had no way out. Realizing the water might rise that high when it was still just a few inches deep on the first floor and choosing to escape to the roof at that point would have made the difference between living and dying. Taking a gallon of white paint and a paintbrush to write, "HELP!" or, "SOS!" on the roof would have been an amazing foresight.

- **Be patient.** Say you are on top of your roof and your neighborhood is now a lake. You have been there for ten hours, and you have not seen any sign of help. The water is over ten feet deep with debris floating everywhere. There are also poisonous snakes now swimming for their lives. If you decide you have had enough of waiting it out on the roof, and you're going to swim for it, it could be a fatal mistake. Suppose you see that two hundred yards away, there is a spot with no flooding. A police van giving care and assistance is nearby. Assuming you were in relatively good health and fitness, it might be reasonable for you to swim. But unless there is a reasonable chance for self-rescue, you are better off waiting in a place where searchers would be expecting you to be.

Applying the Lessons

How can we relate a natural disaster such as Katrina to a more mundane "crisis" that might occur at your business or in your personal life?

Let's follow the same format as above:

- **Don't get in a position where you need to be rescued.** We know we should be doing a number of things from a preventative standpoint, like making periodic data backups, replacing batteries in smoke detectors, creating and testing an evacuation plan, or cross-training employees. Yet these are commonly ignored ... until a disaster occurs. If a pipe breaks and water pours on your server, but you have a backup server and a data backup, it's an inconvenience, not a disaster. If a key employee is hit by a bus,[11] and you have people cross-trained to pick up the slack, then it's not a disaster (except, of course, for the employee!). Diligently performing these preventative tasks and avoiding disaster is relatively easy to do and much, much cheaper than paying for a disaster

- **When a rescue option comes along, take it.** Most people have a natural tendency to politely refuse help. Consider this scenario: you're at work, struggling with an Excel problem, and

---

11 Why is it always "hit by a bus"? The number of people hit by cars is much higher.

it's really frustrating you. Another co-worker says something like, "Hey, you doing okay? Can I help you with anything?" Although you really need the help, you say something like, "No thanks. I got this."

Why is it so hard for us to accept help when help is offered? Some people have a hero complex; they can do everything and need no one's help. Others are naturally shy and feel it would be an imposition. Most frequently, it may be that someone doesn't want to be in another person's debt. (Let's face it. Sometimes, you ask for a ride to the airport and, the next thing you know, you are moving heavy furniture up three flights of stairs.) But we are talking about people who are offering help, not you going around begging for it. When you're in a much more serious situation than figuring out a spreadsheet formula, and someone offers to help (someone you reasonably expect would actually be helpful), accept the help! At least hear them out and decide if the advice or assistance works for your particular situation.

- **Be resourceful.** Do you remember the TV show MacGyver? MacGyver was a secret agent who didn't carry a gun. When he found himself in a tight spot, he used whatever was at hand— duct tape or a paperclip could become the very tool he needed to extract himself. This show spawned a verb, MacGyvering, meaning being resourceful and thinking of innovative solutions with what you have at hand. You are not going to fashion a paperclip and duct tape into a replacement hard disk, but you could use duct tape to hold together a broom and a yardstick that holds the drop ceiling from falling down on employees' heads. (I know this one from experience!) Be on the lookout for solutions that may not be immediately apparent and, more importantly, train yourself to specifically look for MacGyvering opportunities in a crisis. Here are some tips to achieving MacGyver-like resourcefulness status:

- Ask these questions:[12]

  o Is there another way to get what I want?

  o Is the desired result really the best result?

  o Who else has information that might help me?

  o What is something very similar to what I need that might also work?

  o Who is the expert in this area?

  o What is one more thing I can try?

  o What would someone I admire do in this same situation? *(WWMD-What Would MacGyver Do?)*

Speaking of MacGyvering, I had a "near disaster" a couple of years ago (that could have been much worse). I was working in my office and enjoying a glass of ice water. I placed the glass on top of a folded paper towel on top of a coaster. Well, when I took a drink and put the glass back down, I placed it in the center of the paper towel, which had shifted and was no longer in the center of the coaster. I wound up setting the glass on the edge of the coaster. As soon as I let go, the nearly full glass tipped over directly onto my laptop.

Adrenaline rush! This occurred when I was creating an incredibly complex report in a legal case for which I was retained as an expert witness. The timing of this could not have been worse. When you live in Hahira, GA, you do not have an Apple Store right down the street! However, I had prepared in specific ways before this event that helped me immensely. I had immediate access to resources that told what to do when you spill water on your laptop, in this case a MacBook. I did not spend ten minutes fussing and fretting about this water on my laptop.

12 See the origin of these great questions here: http://www.lifehack.org/articles/featured/how-to-promote-resourcefulness-in-yourself-and-others.html

Using my iPhone, I accessed a copy of an article from the Apple support website that explained what to do if your Mac gets wet. The advice is similar to aiding a stroke victim in that, if you do certain things immediately, then you have a greater chance of saving functionality. I quickly grabbed an old towel and turned my laptop upside down on that towel. Also, I had encouraged my wife, Samantha, to buy a Mac, so I would be able to use her Mac as a backup in case of an emergency. In addition, I had a backup of my files.

Three mitigating factors kept this water spill from being a total disaster:

1. I took immediate action to remediate the spill.

2. I had access to a backup computer.

3. More importantly, I actually had a recent backup.

It took several days for my MacBook to return to full functioning status, but I was able to continue working during that time. Offering an excuse, such as "My computer is not working," is not a strategy.

- **Be patient.** This one is hard. The urge to take some action, any action, is strong. Earlier, I talked about taking a supposed corrective action that actually takes you further away from true resolution. Strive to think hard about solutions, decide on a plan, put the plan in place, and wait patiently for the results. You can plan for alternative solutions in case the original plan doesn't work out. There are occasionally situations where multiple solutions can run in parallel. However, by and large, solutions need a reasonable amount of time to be successful before being abandoned.

A Turning Point

The *Grafton* survivors were patient, to a point. As the four-month time frame passed, they thought their rescue was imminent. But the rescue ship never came. After six months passed, they concluded that, most likely, Uncle Musgrave and Sarpy didn't alert the government, or perhaps the rescue ship went to Campbell Island and didn't come to Auckland Island.

So, they enacted several rescue options. There was a tall bluff overlooking their location where the *Grafton* crew could climb up and watch for ships. If they saw a ship, they had a bonfire prepared in order to signal that ship. They also set up a signal flag. The point is, they no longer assumed a ship would be headed directly to Auckland Island but would be sailing by, and sailing by at some distance. If the men were in their cabin or in the woods hunting, they wouldn't see it. If they were looking, the total amount of time a ship would be in view might be an hour or less. It might sail into view in thirty minutes and then go on. So, they regularly went up to this tall point where they could see for quite some distance and scanned the ocean for ships. If anyone saw a ship, he would immediately light the signal fire, which would send up a big, tall plume of smoke.

While maritime law does not specify an absolute requirement that sailors pick up potential shipwreck survivors, there is a strong incentive to do so. As all seafaring crews well understand, the chances they may be castaways themselves at some point provides strong incentive to pick up any they encounter. Maritime law does account for property lost at sea and rescued by another. In that case, the rescuer is entitled to claim an award on the salvaged property, but there is no "life salvage." All mariners are expected to save the lives of others in peril without expectation of reward.

If a passing ship saw a signal, there is a strong possibility the ship would stop and rescue those people. So, Captain Musgrave set up a watch, and each of the five rotated going up to the bluff to search for ships. After doing this faithfully for some months, however, they stopped executing a watch on a regular basis. They grew complacent. They got to the point where they thought, "This is just futile. We're not going to spot a passing ship." They weren't as diligent as they should have been.

Lighting the Rescue Fire

On the other side of Auckland Island, the remaining crew of the *Invercauld* was also trying to survive. Only Captain Dalgarno, First Mate Smith, and Holding, the seaman who was doing everything he could to keep the other guys alive (and who was the true leader of this group), were left. Dalgarno and Smith were doing very little. They were still acting as Holding's superiors. Holding had set up a signal fire should there be an option to hail a passing ship.

One day, he was coming back from a hunting expedition, and Dalgarno was on the shore shouting, "A ship! A ship!" They lit the signal fire, and this big plume of smoke went up. They waited. Would the people on board notice the smoke? If they noticed the smoke, would they stop or continue on?

There were some anxious moments when it seemed the ship would pass on. But, two important things happened. They heard a gunshot fired from the ship, and they could see a boat being lowered and coming toward them. They knew they were going to be rescued! The smaller boat came toward them while the ship continued on to the original settlement, called Port Ross. The ship anchored there, and the smaller boat came for them.

The boat finally reached them as the sun was setting. They realized it was too late to get in the boat and meet up with the other ship. The three men who came on this rescue boat wound up having to spend the night in the cramped, little sod hut the three castaways had set up. The next morning, they rowed to the Spanish ship *Julian*. After a few days, the *Julian* weighed anchor and set off again, heading to Peru, South America. Regardless of the destination, the three men were at last rescued.

Don't Just Sail On

Here's an interesting point: the *Julian* sailed away from Port Ross and never ventured around the island to look for any other survivors. Had they done so, they perhaps would have seen the signal flag of the crew of the *Grafton*. Certainly they would have been in a position for the survivors of the *Grafton* to see them and light their own signal fire. But, they didn't do that. They simply sailed on.

Consider the Goldleaf experience with our "death-spiral" slowness issue. Once we determined the cause of that disaster, we fixed it. But we didn't just "sail on." We went back through the code and the database, scouring them for any similar issue that may have been present. While we found nothing of the potential magnitude of the issue we had faced, we did find several additional areas where our code and database were "sloppy." We were able to fix those, eliminating them as potential problems that could pop up in the future. Had we made the primary fix, given a collective, "Phew, I'm glad that's over!" and gone on about our business, it's possible that our code or database sloppiness could have been a time bomb waiting to go off. And trust me, while our customers gave us a lot of grace over this issue, they would not have borne well having a similar issue appear in subsequent months.

Stay on Watch

It's clear from the historical record that all five *Grafton* survivors were focused on getting the boat prepared for all five to leave Auckland Island. But was this the smartest decision from a "being rescued" standpoint? If you are a castaway, particularly if you are not alone, you should have somebody on watch at all times. The *Grafton* survivors were all-hands-on-deck either forging the nails, bolts, and tools they needed to build the ship, constructing the ship, or hunting for food. They were all engrossed in these tasks. It's not hard to understand why they considered those activities more important than looking for a ship. They were all actively working, and nobody was up at the bluff scanning the horizon. Had they had somebody up there looking, maybe they would have seen the *Julian*.

They could have said, "Okay. We have five men. Four of us will work on the ship, but one is going to be up there looking for other ships." There is a strong possibility they would have seen the *Julian*, not necessarily when it was anchored at Port Ross but certainly as it was coming in or going away from the island. They would have had that 360-degree view of the ocean for quite some distance.

It's interesting to me that this industrious group, who was so busy working at being rescued, missed an opportunity for rescue. They were not diligent in keeping a watch. I think a learning lesson for us is, if there is a reasonable chance for rescue, we shouldn't abandon that, even though we might be actively working on self-rescue.

Using this example, it doesn't seem unreasonable for one person to be on watch while the others work on the ship. As I have previously stated, if there are multiple options that could potentially help in terms of mitigating a problem, and if you have sufficient crew to do so, don't take everybody and put them all on one solution. Split them up. "These six people will work on the primary solution, but one person each will also look at these three other areas because there are some additional possibilities to explore." Don't exclude the possibility of other courses of rescue, even though they're not the primary one you're hopeful about. Make sure you have people assigned to be "on watch" for other options.

A Difficult Choice

The launch and subsequent trial sail of the *Rescue* highlights another great example of leadership from the perspective of providing the best scenario for rescue. Musgrave realized if he dealt with the situation democratically, and they all elected to go, then it would not just be likely they would drown, they would definitely all drown. He could tell the chances for success were very low. He chose two to stay and took two with him in the attempt to get to New Zealand. He knew there was a greater chance for George and Henry to be rescued *if they were left behind*.

Think about that. What if you were in that position? Would you want to be in that little boat, braving the sub-Antarctic seas and weather, sailing toward New Zealand with the potential you would never make it? Or would you want to stay on the island? If you stay, and the others make it and come back for you, that's a positive result. If you stay, and the others wreck and die, then you are still on the island. You still have all the options you had before, except now you have all the resources for two as opposed to sharing with five. You would also still have the opportunity to search for and flag down another ship.

There is no record of whether George or Henry kept a schedule of watches, scanning the horizon for ships. In a similar situation as the original shipwreck, they had an approximate timetable of when it would be reasonable for the *Rescue* to make it to New

Zealand and organize a trip back to retrieve them. But in those weeks, should a passing ship be near enough to the Aucklands, they should have been on watch for it and prepared to hail it with a signal fire.

Being rescued requires patience, persistence, and perspiration, and no opportunity for being rescued or reasonable attempts at self-rescue should be squandered—an important concept to re-member for a business owner, manager, or company employee, re-gardless of how small the disaster may be.

Earning Respect

Consider one final point: the type of leader you are or what type of personal leadership you exhibit also factors into your chance of rescue. As I have previously mentioned, I am not a big fan of lead-ers who verbally abuse employees or act like jerks. This generates fear, and when that boss comes around, people are on edge and generally don't perform well. If you are a leader and your people fear you, what will happen in a disaster? Will they be focused on solutions and being rescued? Or will they be "covering their butts" as they anticipate your rants against them for any perceived fault?

Musgrave's leadership gave his men confidence, and they rallied to the cause of building the *Rescue*. They accepted his solution of leaving two behind. They did not fear Captain Musgrave. You must build up trust and respect amongst your crew in order for them to be in the proper frame of mind in a crisis to be will-ing to do whatever it takes to resolve it. However, there are a few examples of bad leadership in people who went on to create great companies.

Captain Musgrave returns to rescue Harris and Forge
—Alfred De Neuville Engraving, Public Domain—

I've already mentioned Steve Jobs, who by numerous accounts was a harsh man who demanded perfection of his employees. He was often cruel, verbally abusive, and brooding. Yet, his genius was enough to keep many of his employees from quitting, and ultimately Apple became the most valuable non-energy company in the world. I am guessing there are few people in the world who have Steve Jobs' unique qualities. No offense, but you are most likely not one of those.

This concept of earning trust also applies to other stakeholders. Your customers, shareholders, and the greater business community also are worthy of your attempts to be someone worth rescuing. In my example with Goldleaf, we spent years as a customer-centric company, building up goodwill with our financial institution users. So, when we had our system problems, they knew we were the type of company, and I was the type of leader, that had earned respect. That led to the amazing grace we received in that incident. Carefully cultivate a loyalty and respect by intelligent decision-making and benevolent leadership such that your staff will be ready to go through hell itself in order to assist you in being rescued.

CHAPTER FIFTEEN
Grounding Yourself

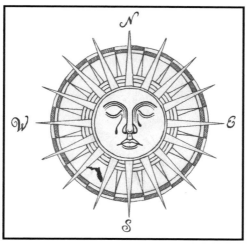

"To err is human, to forgive, divine."

— Alexander Pope

We were able to walk down the mast and onto the beach without even getting wet. It was now pre-dawn. Light was coming up, but it was still dark. Dad went back on the boat and down into the cabin, the majority of which was under water. There was a plastic box that held a flare gun and flares, which were all dry, as it was kept up high on a shelf. The radio was also rigged up high in the cabin and out of the water. Even with the antennae now lying on the beach, Dad was able to use the radio to send out an SOS. Remember this was back before cell phones and distress technology existed. Dad returned to the beach and shot off a couple of flares to give a specific indication of our position for the Bahamian Coast Guard. Then we sat down to wait. It was summertime, so it wasn't particularly cold.

As I recall, we were in disbelief and shock. I have a distinct memory of a high amount of adrenaline running through me.

I remember thinking, "Oh, my gosh! This has happened. We wrecked the Alacrity!"

We were quiet. There was no anger. There were no recriminations. There was just this realization that we had run aground. We were most definitely grounded.

As pre-dawn gave way to dawn, we could see that the boat was intact. We couldn't see any major damage on the side of the boat that was exposed. It looked like there would be a way to pull the boat off, as from our vantage we couldn't see the actual damage to the hull.

I remember thinking, "We'll need to make a temporary repair to the hull, pull the sailboat off the reef, and tow it to where permanent repairs can be made."

We were sitting on this little piece of land; I don't even want to call it an island. Technically a cay, it was really just a sand bar, one of those small cays that's not even identified or named on a map. There are literally thousands of these all over the Bahamas.

We sat there, each of us lost in his own thoughts. I remember talking a little bit about what kind of stuff we would need to get from the Alacrity. Within an hour or so, say around 7:30 or 8:00 in the morning, a Bahamian Coast Guard speedboat showed up, as we were not that far from West End. You could actually see the bigger island of West End to the east of where we were. Because of the shallowness of the water and the coral, they could not come closer than 60 yards or so offshore. They got on the bullhorn and basically told us we had to swim out there, so we did.

We waded out into the water, swam out to their boat, and climbed aboard. From there, it was a short ten-minute ride to the Coast Guard office.

They asked questions like, "Who are you?" and "What are you doing?"

I think there had been significant drug activity in the area. The questions hinted about whether we were involved in some type of illegal or illicit activities.

After about an hour or so, they realized we were just Americans who had wrecked on a cay and said, "Okay, we'll take you back out to your sailboat."

We didn't know it at the time, but there was another disaster in store for us.

Once they were satisfied that we were not drug runners, they took us in the Coast Guard Cutter, and we headed back to the Alacrity. As we were coming around one side of the island to where the boat was laid over on the beach, we saw a small motor boat take off around the other side of the island.

We were like, "Wait, wait! Who are those folks, and what were they doing?"

Again, we couldn't get that close to shore, so the cutter stopped, and we swam ashore to inspect the sailboat in the light. At once, we could see that the Alacrity was completely stripped! Whoever was in that small boat had come and stolen everything: our personal items, all the electronics, and even some items that had been screwed down to the deck.

In no way is the rescue of the Alacrity crew similar to the Grafton or Invercauld. We had modern electronics and were grounded near enough to civilization that Bahamian authorities could easily see our flares. We didn't have to figure out how to survive for an extended period of time on that cay (good thing too as it was a small bit of sand, a couple of palm trees, a bunch of driftwood, and not much else). We were shipwrecked for maybe an hour and a half (hey, shipwrecked is shipwrecked). But given our situation, we did make ourselves able to be rescued by shooting off the flares and going to the coast guard boat when it arrived.

Even after all these years, I still wonder what tipped off the individuals that harvested everything useful from the Alacrity so quickly. Regardless, the end result was that everything of value was gone. That was a gut punch while we were already down. Getting stomped on while you're already on the ground is deflating.

Nonetheless, we did manage to retrieve a few things from Alacrity. The cabin was at an odd angle, so, depending on where you were standing, you were calf-deep to waist-deep in water. I have this distinct memory of diving into the dark water filling the cabin to find my Greek fisherman's hat. A lot of pictures of me from that time show me wearing this very hat. It was covered in diesel fuel, but later I was able to clean it up. I don't know why I was really excited about finding the hat. Given the circumstances, it seems silly now to think that it was something important.

Without a great deal of remorse or sadness or anger, Dad's immediate thought was about what it would take to get the boat off that reef. He made contact with a marine outfit in the Bahamas that could provide boat repairs, and they went out and took a look at the situation.

The devastation was greater than we thought. It wasn't just a small hole. One whole side of the boat, over on the port side, had caved in. The issues were how to get it raised off the reef, how to get it off the island (it would need to be dragged out about sixty yards to get it in deep enough water to float), and how to get it from there to where it could be repaired. Ultimately, the decision was made that the cost of doing all that was too great. In the end, Dad made the incredibly hard decision to abandon his boat.

The Post-Mortem

After a disaster happens, usually there's a time when everyone sits down and conducts a post-mortem, a time of reflection to evaluate what happened and why. You typically ask, "What did we do wrong? What could we have done differently? How could this have turned out better?" Unfortunately, this often devolves into an opportunity for serious finger pointing and accusations. It's not uncommon for the senior manager, owner, or boss to tongue-lash some folks. "Hey! You really screwed up here, and if you hadn't done this and that and whatever else, we wouldn't have been in that predicament."

I think post-mortems are important, and I think it's important to learn from our mistakes. However, in all the post-mortems I've participated in or actually conducted, I have never seen anything productive occur from "ripping somebody a new one" based on their activities or performance. Now, there have been many people in my work experience who deserved to have that happen. I don't know if it makes somebody feel good, or if they feel the need to have a scapegoat, but there is no long-term, positive outcome from verbally tearing somebody apart.

If you need to take somebody aside and address him or her about something they did, then do that privately. If your post-mortem shows that procedures were not appropriately followed, then bring people to task for not following those procedures, i.e., there was an error in execution as opposed to an error in innovation.

Otherwise, I think all your actions and attention should be focused on the most positive elements of learning from what happened. In other words, let's learn from our mistakes. Let's figure out what went right. Let's figure out where we can improve and then work toward making sure that, next time, we resolve it quicker, that we don't fall apart, that we access the right experts as soon as possible, or whatever the lessons are from the specific event. If you can get the entire team thinking about how to positively address the next issue, the post-mortem is the perfect time to do it. Right after the event, everything is still fresh in their minds. People are open to saying, "Okay, we did some things wrong. We needed to do some things better, so let's talk about what those things are."

You can bring these learning lessons home, but not by ranting and raving, throwing papers, and cussing a blue streak. I just don't see anything positive coming from that. So, I'm not a fan of the tirade and would not recommend that the post-mortem be a time for that. (Come to think of it, I have never seen anything positive come from ranting and raving … ever.)

Post Post-Mortem

Let's say the crisis is over. Whatever happened has happened. Let's say you've had your post-mortem. You've pulled people aside. You've given them their personal dressing-down, if that's necessary. You may have even terminated a person or two if this mistake happened multiple times in the past. After all, if there have been previous warnings, and some employees are still making mistakes, you may have to let them go. These are all possibilities. Two things are now very important:

- **Follow Up**— Make sure the changes in procedures you outlined in the post-mortem are taking place. Just like in the crisis, as a senior leader, you're letting people know you're paying attention, you're watching the store, and you're overseeing the execution of solving the problem. You're not going to conduct the post-mortem, then go on about your business like nothing ever happened. You're going to specifically come back around and check in. You are going to verify to make sure those new procedures are in place. So, as your people see you paying attention to these details, they begin to think, "Oh, okay. He's watching the store. Let's make sure that we tighten this up." This is critically important.

- **Exercise Restraint**—Don't bring up the event just to throw it in someone's face or bring it up even as a joke. Especially not as a joke. Let's say there was an employee named John Jones. Somehow, in some particular event that occurred, his actions led to a major problem. He didn't follow procedures. The responsibility of the crisis fell on his shoulders, and he took his dressing down in private. He now understands what he's supposed to do.

Six weeks later, everybody's available for a meeting. He's up at the white board, writing something down, and he knocks over the flip chart. The senior manager in the room says, "Oh yeah. There you go, Jones. Just like six weeks ago when you tanked our whole system." Now, I've been around senior leaders who use that kind of barbing, jesting retort with an undertone of sarcasm. I know a lot of companies where the overall atmosphere includes ridiculing, wounding, and digging as an acceptable practice. Maybe your work place is like that. Maybe you're a senior leader, and that's how you operate. Maybe your senior team is seemingly comfortable with you doing that.

In my personal opinion, I just don't see a place for it. In the example I gave of Mr. Jones, nothing positive will come from his boss continually bringing up this failure over and over and over again. Is that going to make him a better employee? Is that somehow going to make him sharper or better or more confident about how he does his job? I don't think so.

There may be times when you may have to say something biting to make a point. But, if you're constantly doing that, if you regularly throw barbs and jabs, then when it becomes critical to get people's attention, they will be numb to it.

"The boss says that all the time, so it's no big deal."

Now, I'm the type of leader who likes to joke and play around. I like to have a laugh. But I think when you're talking about people's jobs, when you're talking about the seriousness of how employees feel about the security of their jobs, a leader must exercise self-control. I think the senior leaders who constantly throw these failures from the past into people's faces gain nothing productive. It should be avoided altogether.

Setting the Example

As a senior manager or leader of an organization, you have a great responsibility to set the tone for the rest of the team. How you act or, more importantly, how you respond (remember, you are not going to react anymore!) sets the tone for how managers under you will respond. You can model the correct way to respond instead of react. You can choose not to do ugly or harmful things that set a bad example.

If you do have downstream managers who act that way, you can pull them aside and say, "Look, that is not how I want you to act. I'm modeling for you how I want you to act, and I am not behaving the way you are behaving."

If they still continue to rage, then you get rid of those managers because that sends a signal. If you try to correct them, giving them help and management training, and they still act badly, you've got to get rid of them. Otherwise, if you allow it to continue, it sends a message to all the other employees that you're okay with it; you accept and condone bad management.

Quite frankly, the bad manager in your organization may be you. If you're modeling a bad management style, then you can't be surprised when some of the folks underneath you exhibit those same behaviors. You have to start with you. You set the tone. Make sure all your managers know what's acceptable and what's not acceptable. Correct them at every point where they're managing poorly, and if they can't change, then you have to let them go.

If you work for a manager who exhibits traits such as I am describing, then your options may be limited. You can attempt to go above your manager; many companies have an "open door" policy that allows you to air grievances to a higher-level manager. But, even if such a policy exists, don't be surprised if sidestepping your manager has an unpleasant or undesirable outcome. It's likely you could actually make matters worse.

Beyond transferring to a new manager or getting another job, you could set a specific meeting with your manager, go over your issues with him or her in a professional, objective manner and ask to be managed in a different way. It probably won't work, but it's worth a try. If you are considering moving to another job anyway, what's the harm in giving it a try?

The Weight of Responsibility

Think about the sequence of events with the *Alacrity*: we went on a sailing trip, unforeseen things happened, circumstances started getting weird, we wrecked the boat on an island, the boat was damaged, thieves stole everything of value, we found out the damage was irreparable or at least beyond the value of the vessel itself, and then we were stuck in the Bahamas. All this happened within a relatively short period of time, about thirty-six hours.

I don't have any recollection of being in the Bahamas more than that next day. We made arrangements with some guys heading back to West Palm Beach in a big powerboat who agreed to give us a ride. We had our meager little pile of belongings in the back of this huge fishing boat. Ironically, it took us less than two hours to get back to Florida.

I'm pretty sure Dad was able to use a landline before we left and called Mom. She was there at the Port of Palm Beach to pick us up. As we were speeding toward the Florida coast, I noticed my dad's posture—beaten down, forlorn. As soon as he saw Mom, he broke down and started sobbing.

At nineteen years old in the summer of 1979, I don't recall in my entire life ever seeing Dad with that kind of emotion before. I certainly had never seen him broken down crying. In that moment, I had this overall feeling of causation. *I caused all of this* ... because I fell asleep.

The Gift of Mercy

I must point out this amazing fact: at no time after the event, or during that powerboat ride home, or in the days following, or, quite frankly, in the years that have followed, has Dad ever brought this up in a playful or jesting way, such as "Oh yeah, remember you wrecked my sailboat."

My dad now suffers from memory loss and doesn't remember a lot of things from the past. He recently made the comment, "Hey, we had a sailboat once."

He doesn't remember much about the wreck of the *Alacrity*, but in the preceding thirty-five years, when his memory was just fine, it would have been understandable for him to throw a jab out there and say, "Hey, David, remember the boat that you sank?" or "Remember the boat that you fell asleep on and shipwrecked?"

To his credit, he never did that. Never! He actually owned only a share of the sailboat; he had three other partners. He has never brought up the amount it cost him to pay off his partners for their shares of the boat. He never threw it out there as a jab, or in jest, or in anger, or in any way that suggested I was responsible for the demise of the *Alacrity*.

Over the years as a manager, senior manager, and business owner, I've had opportunities to deal with people and have been tempted to throttle them for a mistake. In those moments, I don't think I ever consciously thought, "Oh, yeah. Remember the mercy you received from your dad about the *Alacrity*. Why don't you show some mercy?" I don't ever recall having that kind of truly introspective moment, but I do believe that, overall, I recognize subconsciously that I have been given a lot of grace, that I have been given a great gift of not having that thrown in my face over and over and over again.

To the best of my ability, I've tried to incorporate the idea of offering mercy to people in situations when I could have lorded it over them. There have been times when I could have thrashed an employee, verbally abusing them in front of their peers, but I didn't. Without even thinking about the incident of the *Alacrity*, I just instinctively know that it's wrong. This "instinct" was born after experiencing this mercy, this grace, from my dad after the wreck.

It is hard to understand and truly know the kind of forgiveness I'm referring to. The only other thing I can compare it to occurs in the spiritual world. If you are a spiritual person, perhaps a believer in an organized religion or have studied classical philosophy, then this kind of forgiveness probably makes sense to you. Otherwise, it may be difficult for you to truly understand what it means to be forgiven to the point that the person you offended acts as if the event never happened.

I am personally a Christian, and forgiveness is a tenet of the Christian faith. But you don't have to be a Christian to be cognizant of how you should respond to employees, co-workers, business partners, trading partners, customers, vendors, or even your husband or wife, children, parents, or grandparents. All of those relationships are rife with opportunities to make a choice as to whether or not you're going to bring up a past offense and throw it in their faces or to make a joke about it.

All I can tell you is model good behavior. Think about what you're doing and what positive outcome could come from this interaction. If there is no positive outcome, if there isn't something good that's likely to come of it, then that's a pretty good indication you shouldn't do it at all.

The Power of Free Will

If you're reading this book, and you haven't experienced what it means to have true forgiveness, please know you don't have carte blanche to flame people. You can use the power of your mind and the power of your will to make conscious decisions about how you respond in any given situation, just like the survivors associated with Victor Frankl.

Here's the key point: every single one of that small band of concentration camp inmates survived. It certainly wasn't because of a lack of effort on behalf of the Nazis to try and break them, but because they had an element of control. It gave them a sense of autonomy.

Think back to when you were a kid and you did something bad. Maybe your parents said, "Why'd you do that?" You probably said something like "He made me," or "He did this and made me mad."

At the end of the day, nobody makes you do anything. People can do horrible things to you, and certainly some people could say, "I think you're justified in reacting," or "I certainly understand why you did that." But it doesn't mean you have to.

You are ultimately in control of how you act and react in a given situation or, as we've already talked about, whether you react or respond with a thoughtful idea of the outcome you want.

Being Personally Grounded

In this book, I have attempted to take the stories of the *Alacrity*, *Grafton* and *Invercauld* shipwrecks and intersperse my personal perspective and business experiences to explain what lessons can be derived from them. I started with the idea that strategic leadership and effective decision-making are two traits that make a positive difference in mitigating a disaster. However, after working through the material and continuing to research this issue, I have to understand that leadership and decision-making are not traits. They are behaviors exhibited by people who are grounded.

No, not shipwrecked!

Grounded, as in mentally and emotionally stable, admirably sensible, realistic, and unpretentious. Being grounded in this positive way is something we can often spot in individuals even if we cannot specifically define what we feel about them.

You might hear someone say, "That Sally, now she is really grounded!" If asked, they might say, "She has her head on straight," or "She has the right attitude."

I am convinced that, without being grounded, no one will be able to consistently exhibit great leadership or make effective decisions, particularly in a crisis. If you are just starting your career or starting a new business, you should seek out what will ground you and make you the kind of leader that employees, customers, and investors would want to follow.

But what are the underlying traits that make a person grounded?

CHAPTER SIXTEEN
The Three Anchors

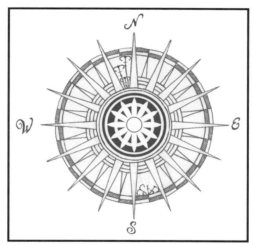

*"Learn from the mistakes of others. You can never
live long enough to make them all yourself."*

— Groucho Marx

My goal in writing this book is to highlight the key traits of strategic leadership and effective decision-making, and how they are exhibited during a disaster. But I realized that leadership and decision-making are not traits that one can have; they are the result of someone who is grounded. So, what makes someone grounded?

To be grounded is to be reliably sensible, emotionally stable, realistic, and unpretentious. Examining the actions of Musgrave and Dalgarno and comparing that to my experience with the *Alacrity* and Goldleaf, I have created the concept of three "Grounded In" Anchors, the three essential traits that make someone grounded.

The existence of the three Grounded In Anchors allows strategic leadership to be developed and exhibited. After developing the three Grounded In Anchors through much trial and error, we become adept at making good decisions. Like a properly deployed anchor can hold fast a ship when a storm is blowing, being grounded in these three traits can provide a stable, sensible place from which you calmly respond to any situation with a proper, unselfish attitude.

You must be **Grounded In**:

Calm Focus

Thoughtful Action

Regard for Others

Conversely, there are three "Grounded By" Anchors—three traits that prevent us from achieving our full potential. These are like an anchor that is dragging in the water when you are attempting to sail on. With an anchor (or anchors) deployed while sailing, you will get hung up on the bottom and go nowhere, or perhaps just be weighed down and never achieve the full sailing potential of the vessel.

Having Grounded By Anchors deployed in your life will paralyze you from being bold and cause you to potentially yield a passive, defeated attitude that denies you your full, potential success.

You must not be **Grounded By**:

Lack of Courage

Lack of Initiative

Lack of Perseverance

Now, let's examine each of these two sets of three Anchors individually.

Grounded In Traits

Grounded In – Calm Focus

When a disaster strikes, you must keep your head. That means not letting the situation put you into a frenzy, but it also means not freezing up. Calm focus is not just being calm, and it isn't just sitting idly by. By calm, I mean keeping your cool and not panicking. The more you are able to keep your emotions under control, the more likely you are to experience a positive outcome. By focus, I mean quickly assessing the situation. Do you need to do something immediately, or do you have time to think, to plan? Are you are keenly aware of what is unfolding around you, and are you appropriately responding to stimuli? It's like when you are in a restaurant, and a server drops a tray full of glasses. Does the resulting shattering noise startle you or make your chest race? The ability to take in what is happening around you and filter out those things that are not a danger to you or don't require your attention is a valuable skill to have.

You can develop this trait. Start by being more aware of what is startling you. Then make a conscious effort not to panic. Yes, don't panic! Many of the negative outcomes in life happen during a panic, right? Shouting in terror when you see a bear in a clearing is definitely not something that will positively affect the situation. By remaining calm and focusing on what requires your immediate attention, you can begin to work towards a solution. Here's a simple but effective tip from Navy Seal training: breathe in and out on a four second count. Literally count to four as you inhale, and count to four as you exhale. This will help calm you and allow you to focus on surrounding stimuli.

Grounded In – Thoughtful Response

Don't react to an emergency. Respond. Reactions are generally knee-jerk, without the required thought necessary to determine the outcome you desire. The following is a good example of a reaction: when someone hits you from behind, you reflexively turn and throw a punch. Responses are generally well thought out as you work toward a specific positive outcome. Maybe an old friend has sneaked up behind you. Surprise! He's now sprawled on the floor after you cold-cocked him.

Being thoughtful means you are thinking about the problem and internally brainstorming potential solutions. It means you are paying attention to other variables—what is going on around you, non-verbal clues, and your experiences and interactions with the person or situation. By not immediately talking (reacting) but instead taking time to think, you can consider a series of internal questions or options before responding. It may sound like that would take too much time, but your amazing brain can quickly process what has been said, consider options, and recall memories. Then, you can assimilate all that, along with external stimuli, in just a few seconds.

Remember the Einstein quote, "If I had an hour to solve a problem, I would spend fifty-five minutes thinking about the problem and five minutes thinking about the solutions." Am I going to run willy-nilly, trying anything to get the crisis resolved, or have I really thought it through? You may have your customers yelling and screaming at you.

"WHY DON'T YOU DO SOMETHING!!!?"

You will feel the pressure to do something. However, take a cautioned approach to any solution. Think. Think hard. Think smart. Then come up with and prioritize potential solutions. Effectively communicate both internally and externally to your staff and customers. Then follow up and make sure people see you actively involved in both the solution itself, as well as encouraging your staff, inspecting their efforts to come up with a solution.

Remember to add into your matrix of potential actions things that might seemingly be disastrous in their own right but may represent less problematic outcomes. In the case of the *Alacrity* shipwreck, if we had motored through the Grand Bahamas inlet in the dark, we might have grounded the boat. Some of you reading this will say, "Hello, David. The *Alacrity* shipwrecked and was destroyed. By trying to go in at night, you would have had a chance to make it in safely. Worst case, you would be stuck in the sand, not wrecked on the rocks."

Touché. Rightly said. While it was my dad's decision to stay offshore, I have to accept the fact that, by falling asleep, I did allow the situation to get to the point where the wreck of the *Alacrity* was a fait accompli; I can't deny that. But, occasionally, you get in a situation where you are looking for the perfect resolution, or what appears to be the thoughtful choice, and you fail to consider other options that may be less dangerous. You know what? Sometimes, it works out. Sometimes you take that chance, and it works out okay. Great! Consider yourself fortunate that it worked out. But, in many cases, without really knowing whether something would be the right choice or not, we jump at an opportunity to reach what we hope is a resolution that ultimately causes more harm. The main point is to make sure that you are considering ALL of the options you have, not just what you think are "good" options.

Learning to give thoughtful responses consistently is hard. Don't think of it as something you have to get 100% right. Hey, you're human. You will make mistakes. But strive to constantly improve your ability to thoughtfully respond instead of react to people and situations. As with everything, the more you practice, the more proficient in thoughtfully responding you will become.

Grounded In – Regard for Others

What does it mean to be Grounded In Regard for Others? Well, it is this simple: don't be selfish! I believe this trait must be present for true leadership to come to the fore. When we act selfishly without regard for anyone around us, be that family, employees, customers, or shareholders, we ultimately fail to achieve leadership in any positive or constructive way. True regard for others combines with thoughtful response to create strategies enacted for the greater good.

There are always extremes. A total narcissist is completely oblivious to the needs of others. And there are people who do not think of themselves at all, completely deferring to the thoughts and demands of another.

Neither of these extremes are healthy. We can have regard for others and still have a healthy sense of self-preservation. If you are a senior manager or business owner, do you earnestly seek out the opinions or ideas from your employees? Even if you know that their opinions and ideas may run counter to your own?

As an entrepreneur, I consistently asked for (and got) the opinions and ideas of my employees. Sometimes I heard things that were hard to take. Sometimes I changed my thinking based on the external input. Other times, this wasn't the case. But I always had an open mind and was willing to listen to alternative views and opinions. Remember, listening to outside opinions does not obligate you to do anything positively or negatively with the information you receive. Just listen. If you choose not to take the advice or counsel offered, explain why, without apology. Then thank them for offering counsel and encourage them to continue to do so.

Now, there are examples of truly selfish people who have attained some level of success. People can (and do) crawl over the backs of others on the path to what they see as success. But, in the long run, over a sustained period of time, people who treat others with disregard get their comeuppance. I truly believe what goes around, comes around. Having true regard for others doesn't mean you are a wimp. If you are a manager or supervisor of others, you must make decisions, and it isn't a democracy. Sometimes, just as when Captain Musgrave left two castaways on Auckland Island, you have to make tough decisions that, at the time, might seem to be less than considerate to others. Yet, as we know from the Grafton story, had Musgrave not made that decision, it is likely all five would have perished.

True regard for others is not always popular; it might not be seen at first for the altruistic act that it is. However, it is always done with the specific intention of serving the greater good of others.

Again, you're human, so you're going to make mistakes. You can't get every decision right. But when you are faced with a choice of action, particularly in a crisis situation, start by asking, "What will most benefit others that are affected by this situation?" Most likely, solutions that work for the good of those around you will also work out well for you.

Effectively cultivating the three Grounded In Anchors will make you a better supervisor, manager, owner, and person. Look around you and notice the people you admire, people you see as truly grounded. Examine the underlying traits of that person and you will likely find the Grounded In traits of calm focus, thoughtful response, and regard for others. And should you desire fellow co-workers, shareholders, or future employers to look at you with such regard, you should strive to develop your Grounded In traits to the maximum capability and intelligence you have been gifted with.

You will not always exhibit all three of the Grounded In traits all of the time. Sometimes you forget one, two, or all three of the traits, and that's likely when you make bad decisions or exhibit poor leadership. When I failed to throw the *Alacrity* anchor out immediately, I had a lack of thoughtful action, which resulted in a bad decision. Sometimes, even if you are exhibiting all three of the traits, a disaster can occur anyway.

Remember the story I told about falling out of the raft and swimming in the Eagle River in Colorado? The bad decision in that event was when I tried to get to the raft to help my friend Chris instead of swimming for the shore. I was acting out of regard for others. But, thoughtful action would have dictated that I go for the shore, thus allowing Chris to also make it safely to shore instead of running another stretch of whitewater unnecessarily. As with most everything, there is no hard and fast rule about how the three traits work in concert with one another. It's easy to look in hindsight and determine if a good decision was made or not. But as a whole, over a sustained period of time, people who are grounded in calm focus, thoughtful action, and regard for others make good decisions and exhibit strategic leadership.

Grounded By Traits

Let's turn our attention to the three *Grounded By* Anchors. These anchors slow us down, stop us from taking calculated risks, prevent us from starting new projects, and make us quick to quit if things are not going well. We will examine each of these in turn:

Grounded By - Lack of Courage

A lack of courage is not the same thing as fear. Fear in and of itself is not a negative. There are times when it's reasonable and appropriate to be afraid. Thinking back to the bear in the clearing example, we see that is a time to be legitimately afraid. However, fear that grounds you to inaction likely results in the bear mauling you. Courage means you overcome your fear and take evasive action that keeps you safe. So, what does it mean to be Grounded by Lack of Courage? Most people just hold back, never take a chance or a risk, and regularly fear rejection or disappointment. Perhaps they grew up in an environment where they never received any encouragement. Perhaps all they heard from family, friends, and authority figures is that they would amount to nothing, never achieve anything. I generally find that to be a self-fulfilling prophecy. Perhaps I am describing your situation.

Here's the good news: regardless of how you were raised, regardless of your present socio-economic situation, you can choose, make a conscious choice, to be more bold and exhibit courage. Say you work in an office environment; you are a clerk manning a cubicle. You are part of a group meeting with the CEO, and there is a specific request for ideas or a potential solution to a vexing problem. Further, you have an idea, and you think it's a good one. Do you raise your hand? If not, why not? Are you waiting for someone else to "break the ice" and be first? What if they offer up an idea or solution that is nearly identical to yours?

Actor/Director Woody Allen famously said, "Eighty percent of success is just showing up." Sometimes it is the very act of being bold that makes the difference. I am a big fan of enthusiasm. Poor ideas presented with enthusiasm get more attention than great ideas presented with no passion. And I believe that lack of courage and lack of enthusiasm are related. People with a lack of courage are generally less enthusiastic. This is a double whammy: low energy and little action.

If you are afraid to take a risk, afraid to raise your hand and say, "Call on me," if you're fearful of rejection, fearful of your thoughts and ideas not being taken seriously, you are Grounded by Lack of Courage.

I get it. Things don't always work out. Rejection and disappointment do happen. But you miss one hundred percent of the opportunities you don't take. Make a conscious decision to be appropriately bold in situations where you previously might have held back. Push past any rejection and keep being bold, building your confidence with each positive result. Develop a healthy "thick skin" to those who would ridicule your ideas and newfound boldness. Avoid people who only say negative things about you in a non-constructive way. Minimize a lack of courage, and you can begin moving faster towards achieving your goals and dreams.

Removing this Grounded By anchor means taking small steps when opportunity presents itself. Raise your hand. Accept a new challenge at work. Take a calculated business risk. Speak confidently when the chairman of the board asks you a question. Always be professional. Remember there is a time and place for your boldness. The next time you encounter a situation where you might normally hold back, give this boldness some freedom and begin taking steps to eliminate the specific behavior that represents a lack of courage.

Decide that potential failure is worth the effort to reach your goals. Perhaps you fear the negative comments from others who belittle your hopes, plans, and dreams. Decide that pushing forward in spite of their negativity is worth the effort. Perhaps you fear self-doubt. Decide that you are going to override your natural inclination to expect a negative result and keep trying until you get a positive result. Then build on that experience and start again. It's hard work. And worth every bit of your best effort.

Grounded By – Lack of Initiative

What does it mean to be Grounded by Lack of Initiative? Well, sometimes a great opportunity falls into your lap. A path to success, all laid out in perfectly planned stages, is presented to you to execute. Hey, it could happen. And if it does, be prepared to act on it. But, more likely, you will need to take initiative to make your own opportunities occur. A lack of initiative is what keeps people from acting on a great idea.

Have you ever heard someone go on and on about the great idea they had for a company or product, but never acted on it? In that situation, I like to ask, "What have you done to bring your idea to fruition?" In most cases, the person has done nothing. All talk, no action. Does this describe someone you know? Does this describe you? Any goal or dream worth chasing will involve some sacrifice. You must plan out the steps to get from idea to completed project. That means researching what those steps are and what it will take for each step to be achieved. You will probably need to make some financial decisions about what you are willing to budget to make your project a reality. Perhaps you will need to engage others to provide some resources along the way. You might be working on this during your lunch breaks or in the evenings and weekends to plan it all out.

Frequently, when I ask what is preventing someone from achieving their goals, the reasons they give are actually excuses. An excuse is a reason that we pre-determine can't be overcome, so we proceed no further: I don't have enough funding. I don't know enough about this industry. I don't have time to pull this idea together.

Excuses are roadblocks of your own making. They can be overcome, but it's a lot easier if you just don't put them in your way in the first place.

Initiative is taking action, even if you make some mistakes along the way. No mistakes means you are making no effort; you're not even trying. Think of those situations where you have let excuses stop you, and brainstorm how you could have gone around that roadblock. At the moment you realize you are offering up yet another excuse for why you are not proceeding, tell yourself, "This is an excuse, and it's not acceptable to use that to stop my progress." Then ask yourself, "How can I get around this excuse, eliminate it, and proceed forward?"

You might have to take a turn here and there. It's unlikely your first plan will be the right one from start to finish. But make progress. Press towards your goals and dreams with dogged determination to succeed.

Grounded By – Lack of Perseverance

Perseverance is the drive to continue, to see something through to the end. I can't count the number of projects, companies, or initiatives that I have seen or experienced as a strategic planning facilitator that were stopped before they could achieve success. When we give up too easily, it perpetuates a cycle of failure, making it easier each time to give up more quickly. The language of this Grounded By anchor is "That will never work," or "It hasn't worked in the past," or other similar statements.

Not seeing something through to its logical end eliminates the opportunity for you to learn. Sometimes it's the second, fifth, or hundredth attempt to succeed that achieves exactly that. Thomas Edison's perseverance with the light bulb is a great example. It took over one thousand iterations of the light bulb before Edison hit on the exact combination of vacuum glass bulb and bamboo filament that produced success.[13] How many light bulb attempts would you have made? Ten? A hundred? Most of us would likely give up well before five hundred and decide it was not going to work. What have you started, only to give up quickly? What was it that caused you to abandon something without seeing it through? Could you press through the urge to quit and stick with projects or activities longer?

You will notice that the three Grounded By Anchors are not the opposite of the three Grounded In Anchors. I specifically want you to think about cultivating the three Grounded In Anchors and, by default, avoid their negative opposites (i.e., be Grounded In Regard for others, and therefore unselfish).

Conversely, I want you to seek out any evidence of the three Grounded By Anchors you may have and work towards eliminating them. By default, you will begin to exhibit more of their

---

13 I find it interesting that, once perfected, Edison's early light bulbs are still working at his home in Southwest Florida which is now a museum. The light bulbs are over a hundred years old and still going strong. (Although if current bulbs had that type of longevity, it wouldn't make for a very good replacement market.)

opposites (i.e., eliminating passivity by exhibiting initiative). Again, not all of the negative Grounded By traits are absent all of the time in people who exhibit strategic leadership or good decision-making.

Practical Application of the Three Anchors

Taking the three Anchors concept and applying that to a business situation might yield the following actions:

Prioritize Solutions

The possibility always exists that a crisis will require an immediate response and not allow you time to prioritize solutions. However, in most cases, you will have time to look at some different solutions discovered by you or your team through brainstorming. You may have two to five options if you're lucky. Both having too few and too many solutions can be problematic. If you only come up with one solution, it might work. It might not work. But if it doesn't, what will you try after that? Finding only one solution is not wise. If you can think of only one real solution, maybe you haven't spent enough time brainstorming potential options.

On the other hand, let's say you spend some time with your team. You say, "Okay, we've got this problem. Let's examine all the different possibilities." You come up with ten potential solutions for the problem. Well, wait a minute. How are you going to make informed decisions about the efficacy of ten different solutions? Even five options is likely too many; that's getting unwieldy. Aim for three reasoned, thoughtful solutions that thoroughly address the potential problem. You must actually spend the time to hash out the details of these plans, and three is a small enough number of possible solutions to manage.

Manage Your Potential Solutions

But you say, "David, how can we ignore ten potential solutions if that is what our brainstorming yielded?" Consider how many of those ten are perhaps subsets of the others. Two of them might be similar. Often, when you have a long list of solutions, you can whittle them down to three or four. You're right in that magic range. If you do have ten, and you can't consolidate them in a reasonable or meaningful way, then you have to prioritize them to get to a manageable number.

Very quickly, I want to know which ones have a reasonable chance of success—not just those that I choose, but also those that other individuals choose, whether they're mid-managers in my company, paid consultants, or anyone I reach out to whom I trust. I try to get as much input as possible. "Take a look at this solution. What kind of probability do you think this would have of resolving the problem?" I analyze all of that input, then create a prioritization of the top options in the order that I think will have the greatest chance of solving the problem.

Here's where you have to factor in some additional variables. Let's say Solution #1 has the greatest chance of solving the problem, but it has certain elements that will require you to spend a significant amount of effort or resources to implement. Neither Solution #2 nor #3 have quite as high a chance of resolving the problem as #1, but they are still promising and significantly faster or less expensive to implement than #1. I'm not automatically going to choose the most expensive option.

I would study the potential solutions. I would think, "I'm not going to guess which one has the most potential for solving the problem. I'm going to apply a factor of problem-solving and time, or perhaps even problem-solving, time, and resources (money, people, etc.)." If it takes you two weeks to work on solving a problem, then those are two weeks you can't get back. Those are two weeks you're not working on something else. Instead of taking two weeks to attempt a permanent solution, I can resolve the problem quickly but maybe not as elegantly or completely as I should. Then, in the course of the next six months, I will implement the permanent solution. The important thing is stopping the problem and making sure the system functions properly for the end-users. Stopping the problem immediately takes precedence over a long-term solution.

Formulate a Rating System

Do you remember the situation a few years back when a BP oil rig out in the Gulf exploded? A lot of people were focused on two objectives: stop the oil from gushing out into the ocean and come up with a long-term plan to cap the oil wells permanently. This is a great analogy for prioritizing solutions. "How do I stop the bleeding? How do I stem the free flow of oil?" Once that has been accomplished, you can ask, "What will I do to create a longer-lasting, hopefully permanent, solution now that I actually have time to think of three or four options?" One of the most important things you can do, then, is come up with solutions you think have potential efficacy towards mitigating the problem with the time you have, and then factor in some kind of rating method to evaluate the potential of this solution. That way you can have at least some relative comparison between the different solutions you see before you. What time frame is required to ascertain whether or not you're seeing a positive impact? How long will it take this solution to show some kind of remediation? Is it working? Is it not working? What resources are required to enact the solution? Based on those three factors (time frame, noticeable results, and required resources), you should be able to see a solution bubble up to the top. "We're going with this one." Once you go with that one, then you go all in and make it happen.

Clearly Communicate

Whatever decisions you've made in terms of brainstorming, considering solutions, and picking solutions, you must clearly communicate these ideas. You have multiple constituencies to whom you are communicating all of this.

First, you're communicating clearly to your internal team. "Here's the problem. Here are the different types of solutions we looked at. Here's the one we're moving forward with and why."

Answer all questions that arise. Make sure you have an open Q&A. Don't just come out in a dictatorial fashion and say, "Here's what we're doing. Get on board." You want to answer all the questions because you don't want anyone to say, "Gosh! He didn't think of this potential problem with the solution. This is not going to work." You want to get all possible input, even though you've spent a significant amount of time thinking about this.

Going back to the Einstein quote, you might have spent fifty-five minutes thinking about the problem and five minutes coming up with a solution, but implementation is a whole separate category not encapsulated by Einstein's notion. Take the time to make sure everyone is clear on what you are planning. Maybe you brought in your managers and spent some time discussing all this, but now you're talking to all the employees. Maybe there's a person far down the totem pole of the organization who, because of her particular life experience, has an idea—a thought, a question, a wrinkle—that somehow no one else thought about. So, if you're giving an update on a solution and asking for feedback, your people will feel the freedom to come forward with an idea you missed, that you didn't think about. Make sure you take the time to clearly communicate and get as much feedback as possible.

Ask questions like:

"Does anybody have any questions?"

"Does anybody have any concerns about whether or not this would actually be effective?"

"Is there anyone who can think of a way we could augment this or do this better or have an idea we didn't consider?"

Be completely transparent and share why you are making the decisions you are making. It is almost always worth sharing the details of your thinking and decision-making during the post-event debrief session.

Who's Doing What?

Once you've clearly communicated internally, there's one more important factor to consider about your team. You need to make sure everybody understands what his or her role is in the implementation phase. Often, you'll see a leader deliver this message of what's going to happen, but he's not completely clear on everyone's responsibilities. Consider the analogy of a football huddle, where the quarterback is giving out certain signals. He says, "Red 42 Slant X" or some similar crazy terminology, but everybody in that huddle knows exactly what their responsibility is based on the command given by the quarterback.

You have to do something similar here by saying, "Okay. Development group, this is what you're going to be doing. Q&A group, you guys need to be teed up for guerilla testing sessions. Marketing, you need to be ready for press inquiries. Sales, you guys need to be communicating with customers." Make sure all the individuals or groups within your company are crystal clear on what their responsibilities are relative to what you're doing to resolve the crisis. If there will be angry customers or people just calling in for more information, make sure everyone knows who will be fielding those calls, so you don't have multiple individuals just saying whatever. You need some kind of control over that particular message.

Communicating to Customers

That brings me to the second constituency to whom you must effectively and clearly communicate, and that is your end-users, your customers. Maybe you have an IT department within your organization, and your "customers" are the other employees within your business. You might be in a similar situation as I was at Goldleaf, a CEO with many customers using your product or service. Whatever your situation is, either as an individual or as a senior manager, you have a constituency of customers. Clearly communicating to these customers about what's happening and what you're doing to remediate the problem is critically important.

Taking the Heat

I've already mentioned in earlier chapters that, during the event we had with Goldleaf when the system would periodically slow down, I wound up having a series of phone calls. Every Wednesday, I conducted a customer conference call. It was basically an open line, and any one of our customers could call in. At this particular juncture, with all of our different software products, Goldleaf had over two thousand financial institutions that used one or more of our software products. Now, most of those calls had many hundreds of banks on the line, and, often, many of those hundreds of participants included the CEO of that financial institution.

Imagine, if you will, that you're a bank and you're using Goldleaf's software product for originating all of your direct deposit, payroll, and direct debits. You know that payments are the lifeblood of your business customers, and they're looking to you to make sure all of their debits and credits are properly processed. You're looking to Goldleaf as the vendor responsible for all of this operating smoothly. But the software is intermittently not working correctly. Imagine being on the phone with me at that point. You would not be casually saying, "Hey, David. Yeah, this is Joe Smith, CEO of First National Bank. David, I'm a little concerned that every now and then the system just seems to death spiral. Yeah, I was just wondering if you guys are thinking about anything over there." No, no, no. You would be intense, insistent, and legitimately upset. You would want to know what I was doing to get past this.

Be Prepared to Educate

Frankly, a good deal of education had to take place. One thing these bank executives kept asking over and over was, "Why don't you roll over to your backup site?" Part of what I had to do was educate them on why moving to the disaster center would have had no effect whatsoever. And I can tell you they did not want to hear that. They wanted the magic, to hear the problem was resolved and all was well. So, I spent a significant amount of time educating them about the actual situation, explaining our process of discovering solutions and why we prioritized those the way we did. Then, I relayed to them the results of our efforts to resolve the problem.

No Ducking and Shucking

So, you must clearly communicate, educate, and relay information without obfuscation, without ducking and shucking. Many examples exist in the industry of a software vendor that had some kind of problem, some kind of bug, and yet failed to own up and fix it. Let's go back to Lotus 123, the software that only functioned correctly up to a certain point, a certain number of digits. An official responded to the issue with, "Yes, but how many people really calculate to that many digits anyway?" Now, if somebody, me or anyone on my staff, had said the equivalent of that about the Goldleaf problem, I would have chopped their head off! (Wait, I already said I wouldn't do that. What my "Grounded In" self would have done is calmly discuss why this approach to communicating with customers is not appropriate and is not something I condone. Then after they left my office, I would scream into a pillow for ten minutes!) The message relayed by that official's reaction is, "Well, this is not really that big a deal. Why are you customers whining about this?" When you have a problem, you stand up, you own up, you emit empathy, you tell them what you're doing to resolve the problem, and you stay in constant communication in appropriate ways with your customer base. They don't have to come find you, seek you out, or chase you down to connect with you. That's effective communication.

Ensure Execution

Okay, you've come up with a solution and effectively communicated it to your staff, stating clearly what you want done.

Now, one option is for you to go away and assume it's done. Probably the funniest example of this leadership style I can think of is in the movie, *Austin Powers*. If you remember, Mike Meyers came up with this character, Austin Powers, who was a caricature of the British spy. In that movie, he also played the alter ego, Dr. Evil, a parody of the bad guy prototype. Well, Dr. Evil eventually puts Austin Powers in mortal danger. He's lowering him into the water with "ill-tempered mutated sea bass" swimming around.

"Start the unnecessarily slow dipping mechanism."

Dr. Evil's son says, "Why don't you go get a gun and shoot him?"

Dr. Evil says, "No, Scotty, no."

"Aren't you gonna go back and look and see if he's dead?" his son asks.

"No, I just assume it's done. What? I don't have to go check."

That to me is the ultimate example of this idea that you would initiate a solution and then just assume your team executed it without any oversight.

Be Present. Be Seen.

As a CEO, I'm not a look-over-your-shoulder-all-the-time guy. If you're my employee, I want to clearly give you my expectations. I will listen to any feedback and then try to remove roadblocks for you, making sure you have all the tools you need to be successful. I want to stay out of your way, unless you have a question. But a time of crisis is not a time for me to be absent.

This is when I need to be visible. Employees and customers need to see me making inquiries, asking about and encouraging and assisting in whatever way possible to make this solution work.

Sometimes it's simple. Sometimes it's just a matter of knowing your people are working late, and bringing in boxes of pizza or snacks. Hey, they're working late, burning the midnight oil, trying to fix this, and I'm right in there with them, right? That simple act says a lot; it's showing regard for others. When I have the opportunity and at an appropriate time, I'll ask, "How are we doing? What specific advancements have we made on this element of the solution? Do we have any idea? What are you seeing?"

Trust and Verify

When people hear me actively asking those questions, I hope it reminds them of Ronald Reagan's famous phrase, "Trust and verify."

I trust these people I've carefully hired and put in place, and they're going to do their job. But, I'm also going to verify. I'm going to follow up. I'm in a position to see and be seen by everyone.

Not only do they know I care, but they also know I'm going to come around and check up on things, so they ought to be working. They ought to be making progress. Say I check on somebody's progress, and they say, "No, we haven't progressed any further." I'll say, "Well, wait a minute. It's been six hours. What's happened in the past six hours?" I'm holding people accountable. I'm saying in so many words, "This work is important. This is critically important to our customers, and we're not making any progress on it."

It tends to keep people on their toes and say, "I know David's going to come around. I know the CEO's going to come around. I know the senior manager's going to come around. My boss is going to come around. I better have some solution. I better show how we're working on things."

Following up and being actively involved adds a little urgency.[14]

Head vs. Heart

You have to be objective in a crisis. You can't let your emotions, passions, adrenaline, or sadness cloud your thinking relative to what you should do next. We are all familiar with the idea of making decisions with your head as opposed to your heart. A lot of times in your personal life, you make decisions concerning relationships (or anything very important to you emotionally) with the heart, and you are right to do that. But most of the business decisions you make and a lot of the personal decisions you make about jobs or how you deal with your boss or other co-workers are decisions best made with your head.

You can introspectively look at the situation and say, "This is the best course of action, even though I really feel I should do something different." In those kinds of situations, it's important for you to take stock of what your heart is saying and what your head is saying. If it's an overwhelming heart thing, and your head says, "Well, I don't feel strongly one way or the other," then feel free to go with your heart. If your head is telling you to do something, and you're earnestly thinking it through, but your heart's tugging you in another direction, it's important for you to think strongly about what your head is telling you. A lot of times, the heart is caught up in the moment. You're emotionally involved

---

14 Now, here's one little note about working with technical people. Some people don't understand how interruptions can affect technically-minded employees. Say I've got a programmer, and he's heads-down in the code, with his headphones on, blaring AC/DC music or whatever, and he's jamming. If I come around, tapping people on the shoulder and interrupting them, I could be causing more harm than good. If I interrupt them and talk with them for five minutes, it could take them an hour to get back in that groove again. You have to know the vibe of your staff, how your technical people work best, and how you should interact with them. Maybe you're in a situation where you don't have technical staff, but you have people who are similar to what I am describing. Interact with your staff at times when they're out of that focused mode. If you see two or three of them standing around, grabbing a cup of coffee or just chatting, that's a good time to ask about their progress.

in the situation. If you could step back and completely remove the emotion from it, you would calmly look at it and say, "Oh, of course! Here's the answer. Yeah, it's clear. I should do this."

I want to comment for a moment about the concept of a "gut feeling." I am somebody who gets a gut feeling about certain things, and I can say, over time, that my gut feeling is right more than it's wrong. However, in a situation where my gut feeling was the thing that got us into a bad situation in the first place, I do have to question whether or not I trust that gut feeling to guide how I'm going to resolve the problem. I second-guess, and third-guess, and fourth-guess myself.

Even though it's difficult to be objective, it's always good to find a way to do so. In some cases, you have to force yourself to remove your feelings from the situation and think of it in more of a dispassionate way. You may be able to reach out and talk to others who can look at the situation and give you their honest opinions. People who have given you an honest opinion in the past that turned out to be valuable are the kinds of people you can describe the scenario to and say, "Given these set of circumstances, what do you think?" They would most likely be more rational in that decision than you. This provides an opportunity to get valuable input in a situation where you might be emotionally compromised.

So, when my dad acknowledged there was no hope of raising the *Alacrity*, the real impact hit him. He broke down and realized he had lost the boat forever. An investment was lost. Other consequences were going to come from this. But to his credit, up to that moment, everything Dad said centered first on our safety and then what could be done to raise this boat. All of his energies went there first. A truly Grounded man. Only when all of those things were exhausted did he allow any kind of real emotional response related to what a disaster this was for him.

The Rest of Dad's Story

I need to take a moment here to share a bit about what happened to my dad, Donald Peterson, following this event on the *Alacrity* because I don't want to leave you with the impression that he wound up being a bitter, shattered man. I've already shared with you that he never came after me with recriminations or any kind of accusatory language. The amount of grace and forgiveness he showed me was amazing, so that already tells you something about his character. I want to make sure you understand that, even though he lost something incredibly important to him, he turned it into a positive thing for his life.

He came back from the Bahamas and worked to pay off his partners. We were a middle class family. My dad was a schoolteacher and professor, and my mom was a secretary and homemaker. There was not a lot of extra money, so this was a big deal for him to have to pay off his other three partners. But, unlike some people you hear about who say, "Sorry, I can't pay you," or "I have to declare bankruptcy," he worked diligently to pay off that debt. He started thinking about how much time he had spent on the boat and whether or not the boat itself had become too much like a god to him. He had basically replaced his love for our Heavenly Father above with this love for the boat and sailing.

This event shook him to the core and was the catalyst for him to turn his full energies to God. He has devoted his life since that event to Christian service. He and Mom wound up working as missionaries in New York City, helping different international Baptist churches in that area. They became missionaries in Haiti for many, many years and trained health workers in remote areas, so people in that impoverished nation could receive health care in their own villages. Remember the mission project put on by our church, where my daughter came along as our medical expert? That campground was actually started by my parents, and they have spent the last fifteen years developing that into a retreat where families can come and be restored.

While these storms of life and business can be devastating, you have a choice as to how they affect you. You've probably heard stories of people who endured events like the shipwreck of the *Alacrity*, or worse, who became bitter and disgruntled and hated God and the world. That is not my dad. He took the wreck as a sign that he needed to do something more important with his life.

While he was serving as a Haitian missionary, my dad got an old fishing boat and motored from West Palm Beach to Haiti on behalf of a local group that needed a boat. Other than that, he never sailed again. In recent years, I took Dad sailing on a day trip in the Gulf of Mexico (see picture below). There have only been a few occasions since the loss of the *Alacrity* when he was able to get on a boat, which is amazing when you consider just how much enjoyment he got from sailing.

Don and David Peterson just before
sailing on Schooner *Freedom*
—David Peterson Collection—

He had found a new purpose for his life and poured himself into that. He has been an amazing father and an inspiration to me as I've tried to conduct myself in business matters, especially in this area of forgiveness and giving people the opportunity to work in an environment where they don't constantly have recriminations over their heads. Those are just a few of the lessons I learned from him.

Putting the Three Anchors into Action

In the odd-numbered chapters of this book, I've been telling the story about my fateful trip on the *Alacrity* in 1979. Throughout those chapters, I've shared an ongoing narrative about this event. Looking back, it's easy to see the big picture. When you're in the middle of a crisis, the big picture is often obscured; you can only see certain portions. You know what you can reasonably deduce based on certain input, certain data, certain experiences, and information you might have available from other experts. For a sailing trip I planned in May of 2015, I applied the learning lessons from *Grounded*. I flew to the island of Tortola in the British Virgin Islands with my wife, Samantha, and two other couples. We chartered a sailboat, an Orana 44 called *Windscape*, from Horizon Yacht Charters in Nanny Cay. The plan was to take possession of her, spend eight days on the water, and then return the boat in one piece.

So, what personal learning lessons did I acquire from my preparation for a new sailing adventure? What learning lessons from the *Alacrity*, *Grafton*, and *Invercauld* did I put into place?

Hire an Expert

I wasn't that familiar with the Orana 44, so I wasn't just going to take possession of it and think, "I've got this." I'm handing over my credit card and signing the waivers, so they're fine for me to charter this sailboat because I'm buying insurance. I didn't want to rely on that because the safety of my wife, these other passengers, and myself was at stake. So, I flew to the British Virgin Islands (BVIs) a day early. I paid extra money for an experienced captain to come on board, so we could go on a practice sailing trip. We sailed around the waters close to the marina to make sure I had a feel for the boat. I wanted to understand and know where all the lines, rigging, and instrumentation were and how they worked. I wanted to understand how to operate the engine. I wanted to be familiar with all of the through-hull fittings. I wanted to understand the electronics, the compass, the ship's radio, and any other kind of navigation equipment on board. We practiced anchoring. We practiced hooking up to a mooring ball. We practiced sailing maneuvers and docking.

All of these things are a little bit different on every boat, so I availed myself of this captain's expertise. Also, I took a log to write detailed notes while the captain was talking. Often on rental sailboats, the lines are color-coded. There might be a line with a yellow fiber running through it, one with a green fiber and one with a red fiber. I needed to instantly know what those lines were and what they did, so if I were pulling on one (or needed to pull on one), I'd know for sure where it went and what it did. If the winds kick up real high, you can reef the mainsail, so less sail would be in use. Well, reefing the mainsail is a little bit different on every sailboat. I made sure I knew and understood how to reef those sails, so we could still sail in a situation with high winds.

This idea of hiring an expert, in advance, to help me understand and familiarize myself with this new vessel was very important. How might you use this principle in operating your business or division?

Diligently Prepare

The BVIs are known as the Disney World of the Caribbean. This is not exactly a difficult area to sail. It's extremely well-charted and you're never out of sight of land. Because I've been there before and have notes about all the different things I did on previous trips, I had a fair amount of knowledge about the BVIs. I felt confident in my ability to navigate the journey I was about to take, but at the same time it wasn't like I'd done this thirty, or even a dozen times (which might have enabled me to expect things to happen a certain way). I was still hyperaware of things that could happen. I wasn't going to rely on any knowledge storehouse of having done this dozens of times. I wouldn't be operating on autopilot. I was on the lookout for potential Black Swan events. The guide books I had read go into detail about where shallow waters are, where I could pick up mooring balls, why I would not want to go a particular way around an island, and why I needed to watch out for that shallow sunken wreck at a specific GPS location. Electronic charts contain all this information, but it's always good to have other reference materials for reinforcement.

Each day, before I pulled up anchor or unhooked from the moor, I had a complete and detailed sailing plan for that day. I knew exactly where I was going, what sailing headings I was going to make. I'd gauge the wind strength and direction, and decide whether I could set a direct course or whether I'd have to tack back and forth. Despite the plan, sometimes we would deviate from it. (Hey, we're chartering a sailboat in the Caribbean. We get to say, "Let's go over there," and do so). But then, once we finished with that little excursion, I would make a new plan and execute it. I wasn't sailing by the seat of my pants. I had detailed, written instructions about what I wanted to do, headings, speed, and wind conditions. I looked at tides, currents, the layout of the islands, the whole nine yards.

About a hundred hours of planning and preparation went into this particular trip. How much time in planning and preparation have you done for the next big upgrade or change in your company? How much time in planning and preparation have you done in advance of a disaster that you can't predict?

Choose the Crew Wisely

Samantha, my wife, has been sailing with me multiple times. In fact, right after I earned my mono-hull captain's license, she and I took a sailing trip on the west coast of Florida. We planned to sail around the St. Petersburg Bay, spend the night anchored, and then come back. We weren't even going out into the Gulf of Mexico. It was a blustery day. Even in the bay, it was choppy when we motored out of the port in this mono-hull. I did not do a checkout sail like I did with the catamaran. I thought, *Fine. Give me this boat. Here's this line. There's that halyard. Let's go.*

We came out of the port, the wind hit the sails, and that sailboat keeled right over to about thirty degrees. Samantha, inexperienced and not expecting that, was very concerned about how much the boat leaned over. She was convinced I was being reckless, and the boat was going to capsize. In reality, it would take near hurricane force winds to flip a thirty-five-foot sailboat. However, I backed off the wind and changed my whole sailing pattern, so the boat wouldn't keel over to that degree. When that trip was over, to her credit she said, "I want to go to the sailing school and learn about the ins and outs of sailing because I don't want to feel uncomfortable in strong winds." So, when I went back to get multi-hull certification, she took the basic keelboat class. Now, she has a complete understanding and comfort with how the sailboat actually works. So, on the BVI trip, I had my experienced first mate, Samantha.

One of the other couples, both husband and wife, had their basic keel boat sailing certification. I had never sailed with them before but, from conversation, I knew they had sailing experience. The third couple did not have any sailing experience at all. But I was okay with that. If Samantha and I went with four people who had no sailing experience, I would have been more concerned. I would have scheduled a day sail out of St. Petersburg or Jacksonville a month or two before our trip with those people just to get comfortable and know they were okay to sail.

Remember my mentioning Andy Wilkes, the plantation manager who accompanied us on the sailing trip? I mean, there wasn't a single piece of mechanical equipment that he couldn't fix. He was just super handy. The other couple consisted of a gentleman who had a doctorate degree and taught business and management at our local university. He was extremely bright and levelheaded. His wife is a nurse practitioner, a skilled medical profession. Both Kellie Wilkes and my wife Samantha are smart and capable who have weathered the storms of child-rearing. Considering the qualities of those individuals, if something were to happen, I was confident they: a) had skills outside of basic sailing skills that would be very useful, and b) they were going to be grounded in calm focus. They were going to be ready, willing, and able to provide real help in a time of crisis.

David Peterson at helm of Windscape,
an Orana 44 Catamaran
—David Peterson Collection—

While I was confident overall about the sailing trip (and thrilled about some of the best snorkeling spots anywhere on the planet!), I was still sensitive to what might go wrong. While I couldn't know what disasters might have happened, I could certainly think through how I would respond if one did. I realize a Black Swan event can happen at any point in my life—boom!—a crisis hits me out of left field. I now rely on being grounded in calm focus, thoughtful action, and regard for others, so I can provide strategic leadership and make good decisions. In fact, I had only one event where my Grounded In traits were lacking, and I motored out of a moor without putting the dinghy up. I just let it trail behind the boat because we were only going a few hundred yards away. Yet, almost immediately, I had to put the port engine in reverse, and since the dinghy was trailing behind I ran over the dinghy painter (line). It seized up the port engine, taking us over an hour to get it working again. It also cost me $500 with the charter company to have the engine checked out by a diver. Nothing like cash out-of-pocket to enforce a learning lesson—be grounded in thoughtful action, not impatience.

Becoming grounded in calm focus, thoughtful action, and regard for others is a lifelong pursuit. You never truly achieve becoming completely grounded, and then you're done. With the right attitude, you will be constantly learning, always improving—throughout your entire life. The key is making continual, conscious efforts to improve and refine the Grounded In traits. Furthermore, being grounded doesn't mean you will never make mistakes. Trust me. You will. We all do. The difference is that a truly grounded person makes fewer serious mistakes, having established the habit of putting careful thought into their actions before taking them. And even the most grounded person can still be slowed by the three Grounded By anchors occasionally.

It will take mental focus to look for instances where lack of courage, initiative, and perseverance show up in your life and work. It will also take mental focus to take thoughtful response to avoid them. I firmly believe that, no matter your circumstance, you can choose to respond to events and people, instead of react. It's your choice whether you allow an event to embitter you and throw you off your game or choose to willingly embrace and learn from it to become an amazing, productive crew member who is a shining example to others. I hope you choose the latter. I want you to choose to see things work out for good, regardless of the circumstances you're in. That's certainly the lesson I learned from my dad.

You have been created with a unique set of innate skills and talents. In order to develop them to achieve your full potential, make a determined effort to become Grounded. It could change your career, your business, or your entire life. For good.

how important my dad was as a shining example of forgiveness. I cannot emphasize enough the impact he has had on my attitude towards being a business leader, father, and husband. They are both well up into their eighties and attended one of the very first keynotes I delivered on *Grounded,* where I was able to recognize my dad, present him with a copy of the book, and had a videographer there to record it all. Priceless!

As I look back to my formative years as a budding professional, there have been other key mentors that I must recognize. John Beck was a programmer/consultant who came in one day each week to Simmons Office Products in North Palm Beach, FL, and in effect became my private tutor in the RPG II programming language. That knowledge then launched me to get an entry-level programming job at The Kirchman Corporation in Orlando, FL. There, Bob Chamberlain taught me how to dress and act for the job you want, not the job you have. Some years later, one of the banking customers I met while there, President Bobby Wetherington, gave a young 28-year-old entrepreneur a chance at Commercial Banking Company in Hahira and Valdosta, GA, and taught me MANY lessons, perhaps the most important of which was to plan for far more expense and much less revenue than you think is possible.

Out of that opportunity was birthed Goldleaf Technologies, a small software company that grew beyond our wildest dreams, and touched many lives of both customers and employees. I must also give a shout out to John Riley, a truly great Christian man and speaker who inspired me to become a public speaker. If people say I deliver great content in a fun, engaging style, then I am channeling John in doing so. I regularly use this line that I stole from John: "Anyone can open an apple and count the number of seeds, but only God can count the number of apples in a single seed." Brilliant. John, I am an unknown apple that sprouted from your seed of inspiration.

Finally, to my wife Samantha, who has weathered this journey with me and commands an expertise in the English language that never ceases to amaze. She can spot the most discreet error or misplaced comma. I am eternally thankful for the wisdom I have acquired through her.

My wish for you is to use this book as inspiration to plan diligently to prepare for your unknown Black Swan event or shipwreck, to work passionately to prevent it from occurring, and to remain Grounded when it inevitably occurs.

— David

About the Author

David L. Peterson is a nationally acclaimed speaker, corporate trainer, executive coach, and seasoned entrepreneur. He has spoken to thousands of audiences of various sizes, and his enthusiasm for all aspects of business and finance, coupled with his masterful storytelling, make for events that are both paradigm-shifting and enjoyable.

David was the original founder of Goldleaf Technologies, a leading provider of electronic payments software and online banking services to independent financial institutions in the US, where he was instrumental in establishing electronic banking and payment systems for commercial banks. Now, David is the Chief Strategic Officer of i7strategies, an independent strategic planning and consulting firm for financial services and electronic payment initiatives. Peterson also served as Executive Consultant for Q2, a market leading virtual banking software and services company based in Austin, Texas, where he focused on enterprise-wide strategic initiatives, client collaboration, and executive consulting.

After three decades of speaking and training in the financial sector, David has collected his effective and easy-to-follow stories and strategies, and is bringing them to a wider audience. David continues to entertain while educating his audiences, whether small groups of executives or on the main stage of association conferences in front of thousands of attendees. He is active on social media and is frequently published in regional and national publications on a wide range of financial, business, and strategic thinking topics. Though he has limited dates for main stage presentations and workshops, David is always enthusiastic for new bookings and looks forward to customizing his events for each and every audience.

Get in touch with David L. Peterson

Telephone	(229) 630-1000
Email	david@davidpeterson.com
LinkedIn	http://linkedin.com/in/dlpspeaks
Facebook	http://facebook.com/dpspeaks
Twitter	http://twitter.com/@dlpspeaks
Instagram	http://instagram.com/dlpspeaks
Google+	http://plus.google.com/+dlpspeaks